ALSO BY GEORGE MONROE

Riding With The Phoenix: To Find A New Moral Imperative

HIDDEN ENEMIES OF DEMOCRACY

Oligarchies On The Rise

GEORGE E. MONROE

authorHOUSE

AuthorHouse™
1663 Liberty Drive
Bloomington, IN 47403
www.authorhouse.com
Phone: 833-262-8899

© 2019 George E. Monroe All rights reserved.

No part of this book may be reproduced, stored in a retrieval system, or transmitted by any means without the written permission of the author.

Published by AuthorHouse 01/26/2023

ISBN: 978-1-7283-2455-5 (sc)
ISBN: 978-1-7283-2454-8 (e)

Library of Congress Control Number: 2019912547

Print information available on the last page.

Any people depicted in stock imagery provided by Getty Images are models, and such images are being used for illustrative purposes only.
Certain stock imagery © Getty Images.

This book is printed on acid-free paper.

Because of the dynamic nature of the Internet, any web addresses or links contained in this book may have changed since publication and may no longer be valid. The views expressed in this work are solely those of the author and do not necessarily reflect the views of the publisher, and the publisher hereby disclaims any responsibility for them.

CONTENTS

Foreword: The Best Way To Read This Book ix
Acknowledgements.. xi

Chapter One 1
*A Critical Finding of the Nuremberg Trials Presages
Worldwide Disaster Looming Over U.S. 2016 Elections*

Chapter Two 5
Trump Knows Exactly What He Is Doing: Why He Expects It To Work

Chapter Three... 7
Unbridled Monopoly: The Real Game of the US 2016 Elections

Chapter Four...11
*Corporate Oligarchs and Their Minions are
Prepared to Control the 2016 Elections*

Chapter Five.. 13
David and Goliath: Story With a Powerful Message for 2016 Elections

Chapter Six 17
*The Special Contribution of Indigenous Americans to
Formation of the Unique Government of the United States*

Chapter Seven 23
Healing the Body Politic

Chapter Eight... 27
Uplifted Awareness: Democracy Can't Work Without It

Chapter Nine 31
Cue the Shock: Trump's Next Move

Chapter Ten 35
Capitalism Is Not The Problem

Chapter Eleven... 39
Democracy Depends on the True Conservative

Chapter Twelve 43
*Creative Entrepeneurial Chicago: Antithesis
of Altright Aims and Machinations*

Chapter Thirteen 47
The Phoenix Also Rises: Regenerating Our Democracy

Chapter Fourteen 51
The Biggest Scam: Trading Democracy For A New Strain of Fascism

Chapter Fifteen 55
*Are Secret Actions of Mike Pence Repeating
An Infamous Betrayal of America?*

Chapter Sixteen.. 59
*The American Connection To the Russian Assaults
On Election Processes In The United States*

Chapter Seventeen.. 63
*Democratic Governments Are Forever Subject To Attack
By Elites Obsessed With Subjugation And Control*

Chapter Eighteen 67
*Buildup of Privately Financed and Controlled Paramilitary
Units: Implications for American Democracy*

Chapter Nineteen 73
Robber Barons Redux: Powerful Oligarchs Team
Up To Usurp American Democracy

Chapter Twenty 79
Research Indicates Computerized Election Theft Is
Being Used To Destroy Our Democracy

Chapter Twenty-One 85
Privatizing Our Public Lands and National Parks:
An Assault on American Democracy

Chapter Twenty-Two 91
Freedom: The Main Goal of a Democratic Government

Chapter Twenty-Three 97
Social Security Maneuvers and Pandemic
Responses Reveal Massive Theft

Chapter Twenty-Four 101
Finding Hope For Democracy Amidst The
Current Chaos and Corruption

Chapter Twenty-Five 105
Keep Your Eyes Fixed On The Poor Player

Chapter Twenty-Six 107
Charles Koch's Excellent Plan Suffers A Devastating Blow

Chapter Twenty-Seven 111
Grand Theft Monopoly: The Destructive Legacy Of Zero-Sum Politics

Chapter Twenty-Eight 115
Biden's Special Challenge: The Deadly White Supremacy Doctrine

Chapter Twenty-Nine... 119
Democratic Education: Antidote To Malignant Suppression

Chapter Thirty... 125
*Astronaut's Journey To The Moon Yields New Perspective
For Dealing With Enemies Of Democracy*

Researching And Learning The Truth About Democracy 131
Selected References... 139
About The Author... 143

FOREWORD: THE BEST WAY TO READ THIS BOOK

Books are usually read from front to back, starting with an Introduction to open the author's story and moving forward through the content chapter by chapter. When the last sentence of the narrative has been read and absorbed, there is a short reiteration of the book's basic message and/or a directive toward recommended actions. However, I am suggesting that **the best way to experience the seminal impact of the revelations in this book will be to read the last chapter first.**

After reading and absorbing the panoramic view in the last chapter (number thirty), go back and take a slow trip through the other twenty-nine chapters that were written over a period of six years as new discoveries were made. While you are reading along, try to think of examples that illustrate what you are reading and think about their meanings for your life.

This reversed reading and contemplative approach will provide a historical perspective and comprehensive awareness of the stealthy moves being made by about 700 mega-wealthy oligarchs around the world who are committed to destroying all democratic governments and bringing back "the good old days" of elite status and brute power without the rule of law.

Most of the information in this book is presented verbatim in the form of articles that were previously published by Reader Supported News (RSN). The articles were written and submitted one at a time, from June of 2016 through September of 2021. Now gathered together in this composite volume, they tell a cumulative story of developing views of the truth that were ever more revealing and frightening as new information was discovered about the hidden enemies of democracy.

The ancient fable of the blind men and the elephant tells a story of folk wisdom based on myriad human experiences. It parallels and illustrates my quest for the solid truth during the years since my visit to Germany and the site of the Nuremberg Trials. A poem by John Godfrey Saxe (1816-1887) retells the enduring fable.

Stanzas from the Saxe poem are added at the beginning of certain chapters to serve as reminders of the problems that result from quick conclusions based on limited information. In addition, the timely inclusion of the stanzas marks tipping points when important new information was gained and resulted in a more comprehensive view.

Uplifted awareness based on unassailable truth is critical to defeating the committed enemies of democracy in America. Diligent searching for evidence of who is involved and what they are aiming to achieve is essential. The articles included in this book have resulted from my personal searching and attempts to share what I have learned about the haters of our democracy and their secret actions to supplant it with an exclusive and excluding plutocracy.

In each article my aim was to share the new information and updated perspective I had at the time. There is some repetition as previously expressed truths are merged with newly discovered information to provide a broader picture. I hope that information in the articles and the updated perspectives will help readers to gain enough of the truth to become fully apprised of the stealthy plan to eliminate democratic government and replace it with a virulent new strain of fascism. I hope also that this knowledge will induce them to join with others and create a unified grass roots movement strong enough to save our democracy from the impending scourge of disaster capitalism.

Note: Links to other publications cited within various chapters are not live. Readers may find live links by entering the link information in a browser or by clicking on the links in the original articles at https://readersupportednews.org. Also, live links are included in e-book versions.

ACKNOWLEDGEMENTS

My debt is extremely great to my dearest friend and life partner, Merle Citrin Monroe, for her unwavering personal support and seminal contributions to the articles included in this book. Her keen interest in public affairs, sound judgment, and technical skills "saved the day" countless times. She was there to help me get moving again when I had writer's block, created a "fuzzy" draft, speculated beyond the available facts, or was having a computer problem. A prolific reader and thinker with more than thirty years of experience as a sociology teacher and secondary school administrator, she was always up to date on important public issues. She questioned my 'insightful" discoveries and partially formed perspectives as I was gearing up to start writing about them. She identified the grammar errors and awkward sentence structures in my rough drafts. When I had a final draft that I felt was ready to submit for publication she graciously gave it a final review. Her editorial suggestions always improved its credibility and strength of appeal to potential readers.

Also, I am greatly indebted to my special friend and professional colleague, Susan Lazar. Our personal friendship started ages ago when she was a student in a junior high school science class I was teaching. It continued to grow ever stronger as the years passed. Eventually, similar interests, shared values, and kindred professions brought us together for work on development of the EREVNA International Peace Center (EIPC) on the Island of Cyprus. In close cooperation with native Cypriot, Kikis Christofides, EIPC Chairman and CEO, Susan established a support organization for this project in the United States. She served as its Executive Director for more than fifteen years and successfully led efforts to obtain Consultative Status for the EIPC with the Economic and Social Council of the United Nations. I was fortunate to serve as Vice Chairman of her Board of Directors throughout that exciting time period. In the summer of 2016 after an animated discussion with Susan about disturbing political events in America she encouraged me to draft an article for submission to Reader supported News (RSN). She offered to read drafts and offer editorial suggestions, especially for appeal to readers who might be moved to join in grass roots actions. My gratitude for Susan's expert assistance throughout the writing and editing of thirty articles and development of this book is profound.

For many hours of stimulating discussion related to the articles in this book and the finished product I am more than happy to acknowledge my unusually perceptive friend and long time professional associate Hall Healy. I learned much from working with him as a fellow board member that included planning to represent the EIPC in its role of Consultative Status with The Economic and Social Council (ECOSOC) of the United Nations. His leadership experience in working with international volunteer organizations like the International Crane Foundation, enabled him to be a special contributor.

For insightful critiquing from their perspectives as learned and aware contemporaries who care deeply about saving and improving democracy, I am happy to acknowledge the positive contributions of my daughters, Abby Monroe and Jorjana (Jan) Munro, to the content and format of the thirty articles and commentary in this book.

CHAPTER ONE

> It was six men of Indostan
> To Learning much inclined,
> Who went to see the Elephant
> Though all of them were blind,
> That each by observation
> Might satisfy his mind.

A CRITICAL FINDING OF THE NUREMBERG TRIALS PRESAGES WORLDWIDE DISASTER LOOMING OVER U.S. 2016 ELECTIONS

Article written by George Monroe
Published by Reader Supported News
Saturday, 18 June 2016 18:49

During a visit to Germany during the summer of 2012, I was amazed at how a vibrant and forward looking German society was incorporating realistic information about the Nazi Era in all manner of artifacts, exhibits, museum programs, and school curricula. These media were designed to critically examine what happened, how it happened, and the terrible results. The stated aim was to share the unvarnished truth, especially with young people who would soon become stewards of the German Nation. The hope was to raise their level of awareness so that they would be able to guard against ever again allowing such a horrific takeover of their beloved country.

Throughout the lectures by museum guides and media accounts of the Nuremberg Trials I was held spellbound by descriptions of the evils that the Nazi regime had perpetrated on German society and the world. Included in the presentation of documented facts was a session on things that were learned from the trials. The most important finding cited was that big German corporations were complicit in bringing Hitler to power. Lured by visions of great profits to be made by the confiscation of properties, slave labor, and the very little expense for subsistence maintenance of workers, already rich corporations like Krupps and Siemens had actually aided and supported the hellish Nazi Regime. At the time, I was somewhat able to reconcile this damning revelation with the positive understanding that they were stopped, exposed, made to pay reparations, and steps were taken to make certain that such terrible crimes would never be repeated.

However, two recently published books by very courageous authors have laid bare previously hidden or suppressed information about American corporations that offers grounds for deep concern. Claire Conner's *Wrapped In the Flag: A Personal History of America's Radical Right* provides an insider's contrite accounting of the John Birch Society, the Koch family, and other corporate allies that have been quietly at work for more than 50 years to incrementally steal control of the U.S. government in order to create economic monopolies for their exclusive benefit. Edwin Black's *Nazi Nexus: America's Corporate Connections to Hitler's Holocaust* exposes and documents how, just like their German counterparts, American corporations like Ford, GM, IBM, Coca Cola, The Carnegie Institution, and The Rockefeller Foundation surreptitiously aided and abetted the Nazis in order to gain illicit profits.

Those corporations are still around and doing plenty of business as usual. Their exclusive interest in doing whatever it takes to generate ever more profits for their shareholders predisposes them to support almost anyone for U.S. President who would afford them unrestricted power and control, even Donald Trump. The ugly elements of such a takeover are now in place, well organized, and largely hidden from view.

Hitler captured the attention of corporate leaders by engaging in crass oratory and spouting bold promises to make Germany great again. He skillfully exploited the pain and desperation felt by certain portions of the population to gain their emotional support. His boisterous public rallies were managed by angry thugs who used violent means to silence or remove protesters. The captains of big German corporations noticed his political prowess. They decided they could buy him enough power to take control of their ailing nation and then leverage their influence with him to develop an invincible Third Reich with great opportunities to gain the profits and power they wanted. His rise to exorbitant power was then greatly accelerated by operating a ministry of propaganda that bombarded the German people with lies, distortions, and hateful rhetoric designed to keep them ignorant and compliant.

Trump seems to be following many aspects of Hitler's playbook. He publically calls people derogatory names and demeans those of ethnic difference. He is followed and protected at public meetings by angry thugs who often resort to violence. At the same time, Americans are bombarded with lies, distortions, and hateful rhetoric by employees of the pervasive media giant, Fox News. Profit driven corporate entities seeking freedom from regulation have lined up extensive cash resources and the services of a wide range of paid-off office holders, all waiting to be deployed on cue. Although his approval ratings with the majority of Americans are so low that they soundly dispute his winning the Presidency, Trump blusters on as if he is assured he will claim the office anyway.

Under these circumstances, the looming potential disaster is that the same amoral corporations that aided the Nazis and unwittingly helped to start World War II might collaborate to steal the U. S. 2016 election and install "The Donald" as their man in the White House. Repercussions of such a move could ignite a violent revolution that will spread around the world.

CHAPTER TWO

The First approached the Elephant
And, happening to fall
Against his broad and sturdy side,
At once began to bawl:
"God bless me, but the Elephant
Is very like a wall!"

TRUMP KNOWS EXACTLY WHAT HE IS DOING: WHY HE EXPECTS IT TO WORK

Article written by George Monroe
Published by Reader Supported News
Thursday, 04 August 2016 13:45

Trump knows exactly what he is doing and why it will work if there isn't a massive effort to inform voters and get them to the polls. He knows that oligarchs and power hungry fascist dreamers the world over surreptitiously offer him encouragement to take over and rein in this American democracy that thwarts their aspirations. He knows that he can count on them to help finance misleading propaganda. He expects that they will support trickery to steal and suppress votes. He knows that his supporters are so fired up by his heated theatrical presentations that they will turn out to vote for him "come hell or high water." In a science based essay published RawStory August 4, 2016, neuroscientist and science writer Bobby Azarian, who is affiliated with George Mason University, reviews extensive research showing that the unbridled loyalty of Trump supporters is automatic and not influenced by logic or reason. Fear keeps his followers energized and focused on the belief that he has the ability to make them safe. He has unique ability to hold his followers attention and keep them aroused. His showmanship and simple messages resonate at a visceral level. People overlook gaffes and excesses that would normally be seen as highly offensive because of his aura as their protector.

There are enough of these deceived but highly motivated folks to claim the presidency for Trump and usher in a fascist government that will spell the end of free America. Unaware but highly motivated Trump supporters will show up at the polls and exercise their right to vote while unwittingly enabling a dictator who will move quickly to institute fascistic reforms. His appointments of justices to the Supreme Court will be the nails in the coffin that eradicate the final traces of our precious democracy.

Highly committed Trump supporters will come out and vote for him in very large numbers. The only way to avoid disaster is for many more people to vote for Hillary Clinton and her compatriots. Those who know what's at stake must offer to share it with those who aren't so well informed. The polls must be manned with trustworthy and caring progressives. Miles must be walked and doorbells must be rung. Rides to the polls must be offered to those who need them. Neighborhood rallies and block parties must be held to educate and energize those who are disconnected or distracted. The enormous effort that went into the first election of President Obama must be revived and expanded. The level of that effort must be topped this time to gain a President and enough members of congress to support a government of, by, and for the people of the United States of America. That's it. Disaster or Better (than ever) days. Your choice.

CHAPTER THREE

UNBRIDLED MONOPOLY: THE REAL GAME OF THE US 2016 ELECTIONS

Article written by George Monroe
Published by Reader Supported News
Friday, 19 August 2016 09:54

The possibility of resolving a wide variety of common concerns is being promoted to the US public as an important goal of active participation in the 2016 elections. This very compelling objective stems from the democratic principles expressed by our forefathers and inscribed in our constitution.

Many US citizens firmly believe that nurturing democratic elections is a valid goal. They commit time and money to help make it viable. However, they are not aware that an elite few of their compatriots have pledged allegiance to a very different goal and are secretly applying enormous resources to achieve it. They are playing a different game that is quite simple in concept but devastating in results when played with powerful resources and devious skill. It is the real game being played behind the scenes in US 2016 elections. Its name is monopoly.

Get out your old Monopoly board game and ask some astute friends to spend a fun evening with you in educational play. Observe what happens as the game unfolds and a few players "win" most of the assets. Like buying up properties in a Monopoly game, wealthy US corporations and other elite groups have been purchasing power positions in a wide range of government agencies and legislative bodies. They have used these positions to get rules ignored and legislation enacted to eliminate many troublesome regulations. Then they have pushed merger after merger of ballooning corporations to create the same kind of invincible power that Monopoly board game players get when they own enough hotels or utilities or rental properties.

The terrible effect of electing Trump will be that a few players in the elite monopoly game will win big while most of us will get wiped out. He will quickly join hands with other greedy and profit hungry players to move government operations in a hard right direction. Diplomatic relationships with other nations will be replaced with stern power edicts based on military might. When he appoints several new judges to the Supreme Court our dream of a democratic society with social and economic parity will be "gone with the wind."

Now, the good news. The suffocating monopolies being sought by the 1% can be avoided. In a groundbreaking book entitled, *The New Golden Age: The Coming Revolution Against Political Corruption and Economic Chaos,* economist and social researcher Ravi Batra identified inevitable cycles through which every society evolves. He offered firm evidence that our US society is nearing the end of a cycle wherein materialistic acquisition by greedy elites is increasingly present and harmful. His findings also showed that when this oppressive condition exists in a society it sooner or later triggers a revolution, which is then followed by a bold new era of progressive improvements. Batra noted that throughout recorded history such revolutions have resulted in destructive violence and bloodshed. However, he offered the hopeful insight that because more people are better informed, the coming revolution in the United States might be peacefully achieved by exercising the power of the ballot box.

Occupy Wall Street protesters planted the seeds for a revolution when they annexed a square block of Manhattan's financial district in September of 2011. They changed the name of Zuccotti Park to Liberty Square and sparked a vigorous movement against the manipulations of greedy Wall Street money-mongers. That movement has continued to grow, especially amongst the educated young. It was clearly in evidence at the recent Democratic Convention in Philadelphia. The concerns and aims of the movement were deliberated along with the revolutionary ideas of Bernie Sanders and Elizabeth Warren when Planks of the 2016 Democratic Party campaign platform were composed. Thus, the stage is now set for fully activating a revolution that will usher in a new era of social and economic parity for all citizens of the United States. Enough committed and active voters can make it happen and assure that the secret monopoly game of the 1% is relegated to the collection of historical failures.

CHAPTER FOUR

CORPORATE OLIGARCHS AND THEIR MINIONS ARE PREPARED TO CONTROL THE 2016 ELECTIONS

Article written by George Monroe
Published by reader Supported News
Friday, 26 August 2016 14:05

Whatever you do to become informed about the real issues in the coming elections, it must at least include reading a recent article by Bob Fitrakis and Harvey Wasserman: http://columbusfreepress. com/article/will-gop-swing-state-governors-strip-flip-donald-trump-white-house. They expose conditions that make the mechanics of this election extremely vulnerable to devious manipulation. They draw on their own extensive legal and political experiences to bring critical information to truth seekers in a very succinct form. Quick and sharp. Straightforward and verifiable. The article is excerpted and summarized from their new book ¾ *The Strip & Flip Selection Of 2016:Five Jim Crows & Electronic Election Theft.*

Besides citing the usual GOP tricks to strip potential voters from the voter roles or deny them the right to cast ballots, they expose how thousands of properly cast ballots simply "disappear." Because the vote for Obama in 2008 was much larger than what the GOP could reasonably steal, he survived and brought other Democrats along with him. The same was true for him in 2012, but not for many of his compatriots.

For the 2016 elections, Fitrakis and Wasserman describe a new and more formidable GOP plan to steal votes by electronic means. They contend that if electronic voting machines now in the hands the GOP governors of such swing states as Florida, North Carolina, Michigan,

Ohio, Iowa, and Arizona remain unregulated and unmonitored, they can be used to flip vote tallies to give Trump the win. Given this state of affairs, getting voters to the polls in overwhelming numbers simply won't work this time. Their voting rights and their actual votes must be protected like never before.

A straight out "win" by Donald Trump will be a disaster. It must be prevented if at all possible. However, even if Trump is not elected he can still "win" big time via the electronic theft described by Fitrakis and Wasserman. If enough GOP minions are retained in office and new ones are elected they can continue the blockage of a President whose power Trump and his supporters want to curtail. If that happens, Hillary may become President and be subjected to the same encumbrance that Obama has had to accept for the past eight years. Under this stalemate situation, Trump and other corporate players will continue doing business as usual. Their profits and power will be enhanced. The rest of us will be obliged to witness the physical deterioration our country and steady reduction of our personal assets.

Not acceptable? Read the book cited above for details about how votes are suppressed and stolen. Then, learn how to help make the changes in voting procedures and the management of electronic voting machines that are critical to stop such theft in the coming elections.

CHAPTER FIVE

The Second, feeling the tusk,
Cried, "HO! What have we here
So very round and smooth and sharp?
To me 'tis very clear
This wonder of an Elephant
Is very like a spear!

DAVID AND GOLIATH: STORY WITH A POWERFUL MESSAGE FOR 2016 ELECTIONS

Article written by George Monroe
Published by Reader Supported News
Sunday, 18 September 2016 06:50

GOLIATH (Donald Trump) is coming. He is big. Very, very, big. He aims to fight us (David) and win. He always wins. We need to be afraid. Very, very, afraid. The odds are mightily in his favor. If he wins, he will take everything of any real value for himself and his loyal minions. Then his elite corporate associates will be set free to exploit the world's resources. People who are different or unable to follow the biddings of the oligarchs in charge will pay a dear price.

Trump's numerous lies have gone far beyond credibility. His threats have far exceeded the boundaries of propriety. He has been sternly admonished for his crass behavior by numerous celebrities from Cher to Colin Powell. The best job by far was the rant by Keith Olbermann on the GQ web show, The Closer. Olbermann recites 176 actual behaviors that demonstrate Trump is grossly untrustworthy and unfit to be the President of the United States: http://www.gq.com/story/176-reasons-donald-trump-shouldn't-be- president-olbermann. However, Trump keeps on pushing the envelope with erratic and ordinarily damming acts. It seems as if, for some secret reason, he is absolutely convinced that his skills and methods will prevail.

Despite his obnoxious behavior, Trump is no dummy. He regularly wheels and deals with elites, oligarchs, and possibly even criminals around the world. That can't be done with only three watts of brain-power. He is an accomplished showman. He can assume and play out various roles, including that of a bumbling miscreant. He has sensed the angst of a large number of disturbed people and adapted his behavior to mobilize it. Using the same tactics that Hitler did in Germany, he has fanned the flames of fear and prejudice to create fanatic groups of supporters. That could even be dangerous to him as the perpetrator, unless he has powerful elites ready to help leverage his win into the kind of control Hitler seized with corporate assistance the moment he became Chancellor.

What are the hidden factors that convince Trump that he is GOLIATH and will be the winner?

- His tactics have mobilized a large number of angry and ignorant people who can be counted on to vote for him.
- Republicans now control 68 of America's state legislative bodies, including 23 states where they control the governor's office and both legislative chambers.
- Most of the nation's voting machines are programmed and serviced by corporations that can manipulate the recording of vote tallies.
- The multi-billionaire Koch brothers and associated oligarchs are funneling many millions of dollars to presidential, congressional, and other candidates who are willing to embrace their self-serving agenda.
- Hundreds of zealous paramilitary "militias" are armed and ready to help "make the country great again."
- The remnants of Blackwater, the world's largest private military organization secretly established during the Bush administration, might be joined with the "militias" to declare martial law, if that becomes necessary.

With all of those resources and his time-tested savvy, it might seem that the odds are definitely in Trump's favor. He is clearly huge. Really, really, huge. As a privileged insider, he would find it easy to believe he is truly invincible. He has overwhelming resources at his disposal to simply squash us without even straining himself. However, we Davids have a simple and special weapon that can be used to defeat GOLIATH'S brute power. We can join hands with our compatriots, move in quickly for the advantage of surprise, and vote him into oblivion!

CHAPTER SIX

All that is necessary for the triumph of evil
is that good men do Nothing.

---Edmund Burke

THE SPECIAL CONTRIBUTION OF INDIGENOUS AMERICANS TO FORMATION OF THE UNIQUE GOVERNMENT OF THE UNITED STATES

Article written by George Monroe
Published by Reader Supported News
Monday, 24 October 2016 03:40

The American Revolution wrested control of the Colonists' lives from the oligarchy of the British Empire. It was the first step in a long and difficult process that is still evolving today. Not every person in the colonies agreed with the changes involved. Some had vested interests in the old scheme of things that provided unbalanced access to power and profits. Under the circumstances they were obliged to keep quiet and pretend allegiance to the cause of the victors. They never left. They have always worked secretly to gain back control and rid the world of this "infection" called democracy.

The unconditional surrender of the British Empire provided the colonists with great relief from egregious burdens. It also offered unprecedented opportunities for establishing a far more equitable system of governance. However, there were no visible examples on the world scene from which to compose a new system based on democratic principles. The lack of creative alternatives had resulted in previous revolutions being followed by more of the same old tactics that were employed by an oppressive monarchy or fascism. There was a severe shortage of ideas and plans for a new government "of the people, by the people, and for the people." Under strong pressure to move quickly and surely, the Founding Fathers of our new republic searched the world over for the information they needed. They consulted with current leaders of revolutions that were struggling and learning from troublesome experience. They were unusually receptive to creative thinking and evidence from sources outside the norm.

The original Colonists had positive interactions with the indigenous natives of North America. Their wisdom about ways to survive under trying conditions in the uncharted woodlands was accepted and much appreciated. Our heartwarming legend of the first Thanksgiving gives testimony to the friendly relations prevailing at the time. At first, many of the pilgrims realized they were unsolicited guests in a land that belonged to others who had lived there for many generations. The early pilgrims acknowledged this reality and found positive ways to get along with their hosts. Sharing cultures was prolific. Intermarriage was frequent. Wise and respected native leaders were included in discussions of conflicts and common problems arising from intercultural differences. Life in the New World seemed to be well in hand. Then, the almost forgotten few who secretly yearned to exploit native resources for their personal profit and power gained enough strength to influence pliant office holders in the new government. Steps were then taken to exclude the Indians from meaningful recognition and participation.

Before that terrible alteration of relationships between the native population and the struggling government, the ongoing search for ideas to help create a truly democratic government resulted in a profound discovery. The new leaders found that a successful democracy was already at work in the northeastern woodlands of the indigenous Iroquois nation. In her seminal book, *Manual for the Peacemaker: An Iroquois Legend to Heal Self & Society, (Quest Books, 1995)* Jean Houston describes the ideas and practices that were incorporated into the design for the new government of the United States of America. Here are some excerpts from her book:

> Together they [the Native Iroquois] created a peaceful democracy among the five tribes of Native peoples in the northeastern woodlands, a true democracy that lasted

hundreds of years and is still, to a remarkable extent in force today.

I believe that Deganawah [their revered leader] deserves to be as well known as the other originators of people-centered government. He helped establish a complex and comprehensive democracy in America long before the Colonists arrived. Proofs of this achievement and stories about him were carried back to Europe by the earliest settlers, soldiers, traders, and missionary priests, and these stories influenced many of the seminal thinkers of England and France who promoted the ideals of a democratic society.

Thus the great ideas and models of democracy began in America with the Native populations, crossed the Atlantic to simmer in Europe, and were re-imported back to these shores to inform and encourage the Founding Fathers.

It was Benjamin Franklin who did more than anyone else to promote the genius of the Iroquois League and recommend the adoption of many of its practices.

Franklin himself never stopped talking and writing about the Iroquois League and the great benefit that would come to any burgeoning democracy by following its principles. His persuasive influence on Thomas Jefferson, James Madison, John Adams, and other framers of the Constitution was considerable, as it was also on his friends and devotees in France, some of which were inspired to consider an end to the monarchy there and the creation of a new republic along principles inspired by the Iroquois.

Despite the seminal and fundamental contributions of Indigenous North Americans to formation of a new government that was for a time the hope of the world, the greedy and power hungry elements of the vulnerable new society conspired to shut off the influence of the "savages" and confiscate their lands. Various Presidents succumbed to the siren song of proposed riches and influence to authorize forced evacuations, seizing of assets, death by stealthily induced diseases, confiscation of native children "to civilize them," forbidding the use of native languages, and exclusion from any meaningful role in affairs of state (except when they desperately needed the Navajo Code Talkers to save the country in WWII). These forces, so well personified by the current GOP Presidential candidate, Donald Trump, have succeeded in bringing our precious democracy to the brink of collapse. They have also been a cancer on the genius governance creations of the Indigenous peoples who so profoundly influenced the enlightened men who became our Founding Fathers.

The current interest in recognizing and supporting Indigenous Americans is more than appropriate. It is long overdue. We can't change the terrible things that have been done to them by the greedy profit and power seekers that have not only stolen from them but from all of us. We need the beauty and genius of our Native brothers and sisters in our lives. We are sorely diminished when we don't have a healthy relationship with them. Our ancestors were either brought to North America by force or immigrated here to seek a better life, away from the bad conditions of life under a variety of despots. For a time they enjoyed the grand fruits of personal freedom and kindred connections with their new neighbors. Then, the selfish obsessions of a few for unlimited acquisition silently and secretly worked to begin compromising the new inclusive form of government. Since the time that change of focus was enacted, it has been a long dark night for our Indigenous Americans. Sadly, it isn't over yet.

Two major happenings in the United States are currently calling wide attention to the conditions that provide incentive for mistreatment of Native Americans and allows the theft of their resources by amoral corporate monopolies and their deluded minions: (1) the attempt, despite their reasoned protests, to build an oil transport pipeline through their land that will destroy sacred artifacts and pollute their water supply, and (2) the actions and pronouncements of U.S. presidential candidate Donald Trump as he has revealed his fascistic aspirations for "making the country great again."

Bright lights are increasingly being shined on the secret clubs and devious plans of the corporate oligarchs. The recent disclosures of their secret manipulations to enact a death sentence on our democracy has increased the awareness of many citizens and spurred them to action. We have begun to realize monopolistic corporate oligarchies and fascism are two virulent strains of the same asocial disease. By his divisive pronouncements and veiled threats Donald Trump has revealed the evil secret agendas of his exclusive and excluding compatriots. His public use of fear and racism has raised public awareness and spurred increasing numbers to active involvement. Thus, the stage has been set for a renewal of commitment to the democratic principles of governance created by Indigenous Americans and freely gifted to the inspired founders of our new republic. Whether this promising move toward healthy renewal prevails will depend on what we do about what we understand as our awareness is uplifted.

CHAPTER SEVEN

> The Third approached the animal
> And, happening to take
> The squirming trunk within his hands,
> Thus boldly up he spake:
> "I see," quoth he, "The Elephant
> Is very like a snake!"

HEALING THE BODY POLITIC

Article written by George Monroe
Published by Reader Supported News
Thursday, 04 August 2016 13:45

Use your imagination to place yourself out in space at the point where Apollo Astronaut Edgar Mitchell once observed planet earth and marveled at its pristine beauty. He wrote that he "had time to relax in weightlessness and contemplate that blue jewel-like home planet suspended in the velvety blackness from which we had come." From that vantage point he was also able to "see" many things not easily discernable when immersed in an earthbound illusion of limited scope. Such a view of our planet today would show that the body politic on our beloved home planet has contracted a serious disease.

Gautama Buddha taught that all views of the world around us are illusions. By that he meant that each person's view of the world is a selected picture of reality. Of the almost infinite number of things it is possible to be aware of, a person becoming acclimated to the world must select a very limited number to which they will give their attention. If their limiting mechanisms go haywire and their senses are receptive to everything possible to attend to all at one time, they will probably "blow a fuse." This presents all members of the human community with the challenge to make a fundamental choice of what to see and how to conduct their lives accordingly.

All of the great religions have posited this challenge in terms of choosing good versus evil. A native Cherokee proverb also states this challenge succinctly:

> There is a battle of two wolves inside us all. One is evil. It is anger, jealousy, greed, resentment, lies, inferiority, and ego. The other is good. It is joy, peace, Love, hope, humility, kindness, empathy, and truth. The wolf that wins? The one you feed.

Sad to say, the wolf that is winning more and more around the globe today is the one identified as evil in this insightful proverb.

Throughout the tenure of mankind on the earth, many dynasties and empires have been created by egoistic earth dwellers who made the choice to feed the evil wolf. The choice was to go with a system of orientation and devotion that was fundamentally selfish. When they were able to convince other choice makers with similar tendencies to join them, aggregates of destructive power were created. In all of these egocentric schemes the fundamental game was monopolistic acquisition by a few and brutal tactics to exclude most others. The aim was to control and exploit masses of people and reap great profits from their enslaved or indentured labors.

Evil conditions grew like a festering boil in the body politic until the pain was too great to bear. And like a boil growing on human flesh, the pain was relieved and healing begun only when the infected core was removed. The mechanism for this removal has always been to activate a violent revolution for bringing about the desired change. Such revolutions have brought down many evil dynasties and empires around the world. Many lives and much treasure were destroyed in the process. However, some of the agents of evil infecting the body politic always survived. They were held in check for a time by inspired efforts of the majority to provide a new era based on healthier choices. At the same time, a few survivors yearned to resurrect for themselves the nefarious benefits of the evil schemes that were vanquished. They surreptitiously set to work gaining converts and stealing increments of power for an eventual takeover.

Such actions are usually confined to acts of war between nations or conglomerate empires. However, two world wars were necessary to cure terrible infections of evil that threatened to destroy the body politic of the entire planet. After a very squeaky victory the winners of WWII convened trials of the core perpetrators in Nuremberg, Germany to start the ultimate healing process. A primary goal was to learn what had been the root cause of such evil and what might be done to prevent any thing like it from happening in the future. The most important finding gleaned from the trials was that big German corporations were complicit in bringing Hitler to power. Lured by visions of great profits to be made by the confiscation of properties, slave labor, and very little expense for subsistence of workers, already rich corporations like Krupps and Siemens actually aided and supported the Nazi Regime. Later on, it was discovered that just like their German counterparts, many American corporations had surreptitiously aided and abetted the Nazis in order to gain illicit profits. For a more complete review of these revelations, see article relating to lessons of the Nuremberg Trials published by Reader Supported News, June 19, 2016: http://readersupportednews.org/pm-section/78-78/37548-a-critical-finding-of-the-nuremberg-trials-presages-worldwide-disaster-looming-over-us-2016-elections

The great fear of many thoughtful people today is that powers stolen by collaborating oligarchs around the world will soon be enough to let them once again start forcing their evil illusions on everyone else. This situation has been made more likely by a serious infection of the worldwide body politic induced by the American economist Milton Friedman, who claimed that his research provided economic validation of the egotistic illusion espoused by author Ayn Rand. Friedman recognized in her exclusive and excluding pronouncements exactly what wealthy and power hungry choice makers wanted to hear. He and his "Chicago Boys" were effective in spreading this illusion around the world as scientifically proven gospel. They educated and coached the brutal dictator Augusto Pinochet as he tried to implement it by "shock and awe" in the stunned South American country of Chile. Other governments around the world were coerced or forced into economic traps that made them beholden to the exploitive power of U. S. corporations aided by the World Bank and the International Monetary Fund. Taking the resources of other peoples by force, even war, was legitimized in the minds of those infected with this illusion. The disease is still growing around the world today and especially in the United States with the unwitting election of Donald Trump to the powerful position of U. S. President with the authority to take over as Commander-in- Chief of the world's most powerful armed forces.

It should not be difficult to compare the chosen values and aims of Trump and his supporters with the goods described in the Cherokee proverb and find them in strong conflict. The same is true in comparing them with descriptions of the good values and actions stated in treatises of any of the Great Religions, including the Christian Bible. The blatant differences that are found when making such comparisons should raise confounding questions. It appears, however, that once the choice is made to accept the precepts of evil, a choice maker is enveloped in an illusion that justifies the choice and makes it impossible to see or accept anything else. Being a virtual prisoner of that illusion without awareness of other relevant information actually makes it possible to rally in support of evil demagogues and vote against one's own best interests. It also induces a kind of blindness that allows those so infected to be surrounded by healthier ideals and not be able to see them.

Donald Trump and his evil-oriented minions must be stopped quickly and decisively. They must be resisted by the same kind of people power Mahatma Gandhi mobilized to free his beloved India from the destructive exploitations of an empire once thought to be invincible. With an erratic fascist-leaning demagogue about to take charge of America and nuclear weapons on the table, the time is very short to cut the core from the current infection of evil in the U.S. body politic. It must be done before the boil bursts and spreads its poisonous contents to create another holocaust and the Armageddon inherent in a third world war. With that much accomplished and unified commitment to feeding the good wolf, the process of healing the body politic can begin.

CHAPTER EIGHT

UPLIFTED AWARENESS: DEMOCRACY CAN'T WORK WITHOUT IT

Article written by George Monroe
Published by Reader Supported News
Saturday, 04 February 2017 10:23

In a democratic republic like the United States, the people organize a representative governing plan to help them obtain what they need for healthy, happy, and productive lives. Ideally this enables them to obtain these things together more effectively than would be possible alone. The men who designed a government for the new American Republic had this in mind. They aimed to replace the repressive oligarchy they escaped with a new government of the people, by the people and for the people. As their hopes for this new form of inclusive government were passionately debated, they realized that there was a dearth of ideas and plans anywhere to be found in the known world at that time for forming such a government.

Expert help to resolve this dilemma actually came from a group of indigenous Native Americans. They had established a complex and comprehensive democracy there long before the Colonists arrived. Benjamin Franklin did more than anyone else to promote the genius of the Iroquois League and recommend many of its practices. He never stopped talking about the great benefit that would come to a democratic republic by following its principles. He persistently brought them to the attention of Thomas Jefferson, James Madison, John Adams, and other framers of the Constitution. For details about this special contribution of indigenous Americans see my article published by Reader Supported News 10/24/16: http://readersupportednews.

org/pm-section/78-78/39867-the-special-contribution-of-indigenous-americans-to-formation-of-the-unique-government-of-the-united-states

From the start, a few greedy and power hungry men in the Colonies were unhappy with this new form of government. They secretly conspired to gain authority to exploit the abundant native resources for their personal profit. Eventually they gained control of enough pliant office holders in the new government to shut off the influence of the native peoples and confiscate their lands. Various U.S. Presidents were also compromised by promises of great power and riches. They joined with corrupted legislators to clear the way for forced evacuations, seizing of assets, and even outright killing when necessary to deal with "the Indian problem."

Under the leadership of President Andrew Jackson millions of native people were forced to leave their homes and land. The folks that elected Jackson and gave him the power to do this were mostly rough frontiersmen. Many of them had served as soldiers in military actions under his command. They had little or no education about the history of the new world and the exceptional value of a democratic government the natives had helped to create. Physical and economic survival at a subsistence level was their main concern. They saw that the natives had lots of land on which crops were raised and plentiful game was hunted for furs and food. Their experience with Jackson led them to revere him as a man of action who took care of his own and got things done. Angry and unaware ruffians voted Jackson into the office of President and beset him with noisy demands that he reward their loyalty by getting rid of the natives that stood in their way, once and for all.

In yielding to the demands of his supporters Jackson initiated one of the most horrible instances of attempted genocide in the history of the world. Information about the brutal methods used and the millions killed was suppressed for many years. Only about sixty years ago did details of this travesty start coming into public discourse. It is doubtful that more than a few thousand Americans know what the Cherokees suffered. Fewer still are aware of how their story parallels the recent election of Donald Trump as President.

Consider that one of Trump's first acts upon moving into the White House was to hang a portrait of Andrew Jackson in the Oval Office. His admiration for Jackson says a great deal about what he means when he talks about making America great again. Jackson's supporters wanted the natives' land and a chance to make a fortune growing crops on it. The moneyed elites of today also want land belonging to natives and a chance to make fortunes with it by extracting underground resources (oil, gas, minerals). As in Jackson's era, this can't be done without support of a corrupted government and lying, stealing, forced transfer, or even killing the rightful owners.

Most people who voted for Trump probably would not condone the policies and methods he represents if they knew the truth about them. When asked, well meaning supporters said they voted "for needed change." They also revealed to the questioners that they had little or no information about the related historical truths, and the hidden aspirations of the candidate. However well meant, the effects of good faith but uninformed decisions can bring forth terrible results. That is a very painful truth we are now learning the hard way as we teeter on the threshold of disaster. If we are to save our wounded republic, uplifted awareness of the truth is critically needed. It is the only cure for the ignorance that leaves us blinded to how our democracy is being systematically stolen behind our backs. It is the only viable means for understanding what currently plagues our special government and what we can do to effect a healing.

A good place to start is by researching the true story of how the native Cherokee Tribe was decimated by an ambitious demagogue and mobs of wanton ruffians who supported him. Also, let it soak in that the Cherokee clearances were financed by a few wealthy men and the banks they controlled. The true story of the Cherokee holocaust is available on several Internet websites, including: http://www.ushistory.org/us/24f.asp. It is also told in **Unto These Hills,** a heartbreaking outdoor pageant performed every summer at the Mountainside Theater in Cherokee, North Carolina: http://www.cherokeesmokies.com/unto_these_hills.html

Check it out. Consider what this information implies about the situation we are in right now. Then join with others who are seeking to uplift public awareness of the truth and work with them to resist Trump's plan to make America (great again) as it was during the reign of Andrew Jackson. While you are at it, scope out Trump's grand illusion for teaming up with other world players beyond America, like Russia's Putin, to make the biggest and best deals for power and profits the world has ever seen. Find out what really moves Mike Pence, who claims to be a true Christian on special assignment directly from God, to embrace the egocentric illusion of Donald Trump whose pronouncements and actions closely resemble the biblical description of the antichrist. Discover the game plan of virtual President, Steve Bannon, who now sits at Trump's right hand and orchestrates his movements to consolidate power. Research what role is envisioned for the world's largest private army, previously named Blackwater Worldwide and founded by Eric Prince, brother of multi-billionaire Trump team member Betsy DeVos.

Make it pressing business to get truthful information about these issues and share it with others. Then find ways to help create the uplifted awareness that can enable multitudes of ordinary people to be a dedicated force great enough to neutralize the concentration of evil in the deceptive plans of Trump and his fascist friends. Keep in mind that there are more of us than there are of them, but that only works if we join together in active combat. We must fight now against what we know is evil and for what we know is good at the same time.

CHAPTER NINE

The Fourth reached out an eager hand,
And felt about the knee:
"What most the wondrous beast is like
Is very plain," quoth he;
"Tis clear enough the Elephant
Is very like a tree!"

CUE THE SHOCK: TRUMP'S NEXT MOVE

Article written by George Monroe
Published by Reader Supported News
Sunday, 09 April 2017 12:47

There has been considerable speculation about whether Trump is a student of methods used by the Nazis to gain power in Germany. His personal behavior and manipulative political actions seem to be following in Hitler's footsteps. Analysis of the methods used to create the Third Reich shows patterns of actions and events that closely mirror what we see happening today in America under Trump's direction.

At the conclusion of the Nuremberg Trials it was felt that the terrible lessons learned from analyzing what the Nazis thought and how they came to power gave incentive to prevent anything like their regime from ever rising up again. Sad to say, the virus of wanton tyranny was not fully eliminated. It was only tamped down and repressed. It found hidden places to grow and infect anew. Its largely hidden but steady growth can be traced in the writings of Ayn Rand, the government change experiments of economist Milton Friedman, George Bush's shock and awe transgressions in Iraq, and the election of Donald Trump to be President of the United States.

Although expressed in different literary terms, the social postulates offered in the writings of Ayn Rand after WWII were basically identical to those formulated and applied by the Nazis. Prominent American economist Milton Friedman recognized that Rand's exclusive and excluding pronouncements actually contained the fundamental aims of the Nazi regime. He realized that the individualist doctrines embedded in *The Fountainhead and Atlas Shrugged* were what power seekers everywhere wanted to hear.

From his position as a professor at the University of Chicago Friedman designed a program to rapidly change existing governments to the free market design he claimed was validated by his research. Friedman and his U. of C. students of free market economics were able to spread this illusion around the world as scientifically proven gospel. They educated and coached powerful dictators like Augusto Pinochet as he tried to implement it with "shock and awe" in the stunned South American country of Chile.

While Friedman's design does work to create instant change that is welcomed by a few, it comes at a terrible price for many. Those who refuse to comply must submit as required or be eliminated. Torture and killing are seen as necessary actions to create the conditions for full and unwavering support of unregulated "free market" capitalism under the oversight of responsible elites. More than thirty thousand resisters were "disappeared" during the guided application of the design in Chile. At Friedman's direction the governments of many nations around the world, e.g. Argentina, Bolivia, China, Poland, Thailand, Sri Lanka, Iraq, and Russia were lured or coerced into economic traps that made them beholden to the exploitive power of United States corporations. He was aided in these ventures by the World Bank and the International Monetary Fund. All of this and much more took place beyond the awareness of most U.S. citizens but has been documented in great detail by award- winning journalist and social activist Naomi Klein in her groundbreaking book, *The Shock Doctrine: The Rise of Disaster Capitalism.*

It is important to note that the ailing government of Russia was among those to which Friedman's "Chicago School" program was applied. The results were economic disaster for most ordinary Russians and exponential increases in the wealth of a chosen few. In September of 1999, the country was hit with a series of mysterious terror attacks. More than three hundred people were killed. That set the stage for a fast takeover by the country's iron-handed prime minister, Vladimir Putin, in the same way the stage was set was set 66 years earlier for Hitler's takeover in Germany.

Both Trump and Putin are well informed about how Friedman's design works to eliminate democratic controls and make a government accept swift change to a free market system managed by elites. Trump has taken unsettling preliminary steps following "Chicago School" guidelines that could just as well be derived from records of Nazi aims and accomplishments. His extreme cabinet appointments, raving tweets, and numerous "shoot from the hip" executive orders have left a large portion of the American public angry and apprehensive. They are concerned that he might stage an event like the burning of the Reichstag in Berlin that vaulted Hitler and the Nazis to power, as a prelude to activating changes he and Putin would like to see. In view of the disturbing trend of Trump's actions Noam Chomsky, Professor Emeritus of MIT and renowned sage, speculated in recent interview: "I think we shouldn't put aside the possibility that there would be some kind of staged or alleged terrorist attack which can change the country instantly." https://chomsky.info/20170327

If Trump does make such a move it will be swift and designed to create extreme chaos. The aim will be to induce mind-numbing confusion and fear. If that happens, Chomsky advises that we must not allow ourselves to drown in despair. Instead, we must stay alert, prepare to stand fast, and be ready to organize our resources for effective resistance until the deadly virus of disaster capitalism has been put back in its box.

CHAPTER TEN

> We can do nothing of good in the way of regulating and supervising corporations until we fix clearly in our minds that we are not attacking the corporations, but endeavoring to do away with any evil in them. We are not hostile to them, we are merely determined that they shall be so handled as to subserve the public good. We draw the line at misconduct, not against wealth.
>
> --- Theodore Roosevelt

CAPITALISM IS NOT THE PROBLEM

Written by George Monroe
Published by Reader Supported News
Monday, 08 May 2017 13:52

There can be no real peace in the world without economic justice. Although many noted injustices and violent wars have had their origins in capitalistic enterprises, capitalism, per se, is not the problem. There are positive aspects to capitalism that are of great value. It motivates. It spurs innovation. It induces commitment. It rewards creative and productive behavior.

However, capitalism that is not regulated by moral imperatives and follows a course of *profits above all* is ultimately destructive. It inevitably leads to hostility. It often results in deadly conflict. It is toxic to peace because it is exclusive and excluding. Without peace, the human, technological, and spiritual resources needed for supporting the good life and human progress are sinfully wasted.

Only inspired democratic systems can offer the creativity and commit the resources that will be needed for obtaining an equitable and sustainable peace. Dictatorships of any kind, religious, scientific, governmental, or corporate can't find ways to make peace because they shut down the free flow of information and limit access to universal truths. Change that is brought about by overwhelming force, shock and awe, and the power of elites tends to put a lock on things and promote the status quo.

Human beings alive today are on a journey. Like it or not, we are all traveling on the same vehicle, Planet Earth. And we are at a critical juncture in that journey. We are in great need of a new moral compass to guide us in making decisions about how to conduct ourselves as we ride through time and space. We need to bring the best of religious thought and modern science together to formulate plans for our current well-being and our ultimate survival. Above all, we must not let a few underdeveloped and shortsighted people capture the resources needed for this cosmic level task. *Uplifted awareness, individually and together, is absolutely vital.*

The government of the United States of America was formed in a bloody revolution. The war with the British Empire was a revolutionary war. Like other great revolutions it was a dangerous struggle against a tyrannical enterprise that was based on monopoly capitalism. Before the uprising to shake off unbearable controls on the colonists, all of the valued goods were owned by a despotic monarch. The masses were degraded and forcibly consigned to hard labor with only meager allotments of life necessities like food, clothing, and shelter. Acceptance of their fate to serve the King without complaint was enforced by terrible punishments.

There were other great revolutions around the world before the American colonists declared independence. However, those revolutions were soon compromised by the stealthy moves of a few who yearned for a return to the "good old days" when their wealth guaranteed unchallenged power to govern the majority of disenfranchised commoners. The founding fathers of the American Revolution, aided by wise elders of indigenous North Americans, designed a new system for governing the United States that was unlike any known in the world at the time. It aimed to provide an effective governing plan for the new nation, including checks and balances to protect it from it from encroachment by the side-lined elites. The founders knew there would always be a wealthy faction working to usurp the power and benefits offered to all citizens in the fledgling democratic republic. For more than two hundred and forty years that plan has worked to keep U.S. government free from takeovers by self-centered despots and their greedy followers. Today, however, the illegitimate election of Donald Trump to the office of President presents a frightening challenge to democratic ideals of governance on which our nation is based. It also has frightening implications for nations around the world.

The challenge currently spearheaded by Donald Trump and his minions is based on the writings of popular author Ayn Rand and promoted by Nobel prize winning economist, Milton Friedman. It starts with the fundamental premise that greed is good. It claims that individuals and corporations have no responsibility for anyone or anything beyond themselves. See my previous RSN article that details how this world-view is a scheme that gives license to defraud trusting people and steal their hard won civil rights with impunity: http://readersupportednews.org/pm-section/78-78/42957-cue-the-shock-trumps-next-move

Our unique democratic republic was once considered to be a bright light unto the world. It inspired the weary but hopeful people of France to create and send us a statue of liberty symbolizing that value in their minds and hearts. Today, as never before, the real issue confronting citizens of the United States is clearly defined. The problem is not capitalism. **The problem is that adulterated capitalism is being used as a weapon for destroying our democratic republic to be replaced with an oligarchy managed by a few self-selected elites.**

In America today, our government based on liberty and freedom of choice is in a battle-to-the-death with an egocentric scheme that offers oppression and subjugation. The primal choice to be made is whether to fight for a representative democratic republic guided by a moral imperative OR to succumb to an oligarchy that is managed by a few elites who profess to answer to no higher authority than *themselves*. At this time, the destructive forces of selfish greed are deeply entrenched in the fabric of our republic, but the seeds of their demise are inherent in their negative nature. With the concerted action of franchised citizens guided by a positive moral imperative, the soul of America can be restored and the light of freedom can be relit. The destructive forces will give way when an enlightened and committed people gather together, declare that enough is enough, and seriously go to work toward a brighter future for everyone. We have the numbers. We just need the will to take sufficient action.

CHAPTER ELEVEN

DEMOCRACY DEPENDS ON THE TRUE CONSERVATIVE

> The Fifth, who chanced to touch the ear
> Said, "Even the blindest man
> Can tell what this resembles most;
> Deny the fact who can
> This marvel of an elephant
> Is very like a fan!"

Article written by George Monroe
Published by Reader Supported News
Thursday, 29 June 2017 06:16

True conservatives are first and foremost *choice-makers*. They try to see both sides of important issues and evaluate the facts. What is working well in regard to those issues, they decide to accept and support. At the same time, they choose to entertain new ideas about those issues that might offer new ways to do some thing better. If the facts look promising, they are willing and able to try a new approach and carefully study the effects while at the same time holding on to what has already proven to be worthwhile.

Throughout the history of the American democracy there have been true conservatives from both U.S. political parties including: Thomas Jefferson, Samuel Adams, Alexander Hamilton, Theodore Roosevelt, Abraham Lincoln, Franklin Roosevelt, Everett Dirksen, Adlai Stevenson, Jacob Javits, and Dwight Eisenhower. Others may fit this definition quite well; the aim of any of them was to conserve what was currently working well while researching the potential of new ideas to improve the lives of all Americans.

True conservatives firmly believe in what they are doing, but they realize and accept that they are not perfect. They are willing and able to learn from their experience as choice makers. At the same time they are grounded by thoughtfully chosen moral imperatives. They have examined the consequences of life as opposed to death and chosen life. Having chosen life, they have looked ahead to examine the consequences of living in creative and productive ways as opposed to non-productive or destructive ways and decided that creative productivity seems more promising than trying to sit still or destroy things. Gratefully acknowledging the unique and fortunate benefits of revolutionary America, they pledge to protect its constitutional framework while helping to find ways to improve its ability to evolve as a government of the people, by the people, and for the people.

Some notable contemporary Americans, e.g. Donald Trump, Steve Bannon, Charles Koch, Carl Icahn, Elaine Chao, Betsy DeVos, Rex Tillerson, Wilbur Ross, Eric Prince, Mitch McConnell, Jared Kushner, and Mike Pence have misappropriated and vulgarized the term conservative. They are not true conservatives by at least three measures:(1) they have chosen to live their lives in negative and destructive ways primarily designed for acquisition of personal wealth, (2) they have decided to ignore the maxims for living good lives offered by the world's major religions, and (3) they have chosen to reject and even subvert the defining features of the democratic government creatively produced in the crucible of our American Revolution. For a candid look at how this rejection and subversion has been operating behind the scenes, see the powerful documentary video entitled, *Get Me Roger Stone* (now available on Netflix).

Their obsession for amassing wealth casts them as narrow-minded and self-centered **acquisitors**, rather than conservatives. They focus on gathering and protecting their possessions. They see democratic government as a nuisance to be stamped out and replaced with a small fascist type government managed by an elite few. They see other people around the world as commoners to be exploited or shut out and deprived. Their loyalty is only to money, not to any particular society or a home country. With parasitic acumen, they attach to any place or group that is seen as a source of exclusive riches. While claiming to value individual freedom and democratic participation under the constitution, they actually conspire with others in elite secret societies and organizations like the John Birch Society, the National Rifle Association, and the Ku Klux Klan to contain, reduce, or exclude citizen involvement in the government. Fake news, fake threats, and fake conflicts about incendiary issues are employed to keep the public stirred up and preoccupied so they won't notice that fundamental rights and legal protections are being systematically cancelled.

The most diligent scholar of conservatism in developing democracies around the world, Peter Viereck, wrote in his 1978 book, *Conservatism Revisited,* that a democratic society functioned best when the conservative liberals and liberal conservatives worked together across the aisle. The give and take involved was the crucible for forward progress and improvement of the system for all citizens. This is certainly the thinking of Michael Bloomberg and Carl Pope presented in their new book, *Climate of Hope: How Cities, Businesses, and Citizens can Save the Planet.*

By contrast, the design of Charles Koch and his followers who have infiltrated and castrated the Republican Party contains the mandate that **no compromise** is allowed. Mike Pence has been a secret leader in this movement for a long time. He is financed in his actions by Charles Koch as are such prominent others as the Governors of Illinois (Bruce Rauner) and Wisconsin (Scott Walker). So are a number of senators such as Mitch McConnell. They are willingly engaged in a paid mission grounded in the self-centered writings of Ayn Rand, Milton Friedman, and right-wing economics professor James Buchanan to subvert and eliminate the democratic form of government to which they pledged allegiance when sworn into their elected offices.

Treason is defined in Webster's New World College Dictionary as *violation of the allegiance owed to one's sovereign or state; betrayal of one's country; specifically in the U.S. (as declared in the Constitution).* It seems clear that many of the current state and national officeholders that call themselves republicans are engaged in activities that fit this definition. The good news is that the true conservatives in our midst outnumber the misguided charlatans who have besieged America. However, there is imminent need for the true conservatives in both parties to come together now and move quickly while there is still time to help the republic recover from the body blows it has been dealt.

Under the current political circumstances, swift action is critically needed on three fronts to: (1) make the public aware of what is happening and who is involved, (2) engage in thoughtful discourse to help find the new moral imperatives that are needed for guiding our choices for operating and improving our seminal democracy, and (3) stop the stealthy theft of the United States government, remove the treasonous thieves from power, and begin the execution of justice to correct the damage already done. A good place to start would be to read and share the content of the new book by award winning Professor of History and Public Policy Nancy McLean entitled, *Democracy In Chains: The Deep History* of the *Radical Right's Stealth Plan for America.*

CHAPTER TWELVE

CREATIVE ENTREPENEURIAL CHICAGO: ANTITHESIS OF ALTRIGHT AIMS AND MACHINATIONS

Written by George Monroe
Published by Reader Supported News
Friday, 22 September 2017 13:17

SPECIAL NOTE FROM THE WRITER:

It may seem that the title and content of this article is out of place and doesn't fit with the other articles that mainly seek to make readers aware of previously hidden threats to our democracy. This article is excitingly different, in that it demonstrates how thoughtful leaders of government and profit-making business enterprises can work together in ways that improve the quality of life for a city's residents and visitors. It describes a living example of positive collaboration wherein people are engaging in the kind of creative thinking and acting that is supported by a balanced and equitable democracy. It illustrates a viable antithesis to the aims and machinations of the deviant acquisitors who have little or no concern for their communities as they seek unregulated power and profits exclusively for themselves.

Despite the daily barrage of destructive pronouncements and actions by the Trump Administration, government leaders of the City of Chicago are collaborating with business leaders to offer support for innovative ideas to reinvent the river that runs through it. An Ideas Lab called *River Edge* has invited nine leading architectural firms to develop and share their creative visions.

The city government, led by Mayor Rahm Emanuel, offers opportunities and supports to the Chicago business community. It expedites trips through complex processes overseen by relevant city departments. It also provides legal protections that are needed to create and operate viable profit-making business enterprises. In turn, businesses put energy and resources into innovative ways to prosper while working to improve the quality of life for the city's residents and visitors.

A showcase of the goals and current efforts of River Edge Ideas Lab is now on display at Expo 72: 72 East Randolph Street in Chicago. The public is invited to view the colorful exhibits and share their thoughts on what resonates with them. For additional information see: ChiRiverLab.com Take a tour through this exhibit guided by the savvy young men and women who have put it together. Witness the colorful displays of creative improvements superimposed on enlarged photographs of actual city features alongside the river. See the proposed designs to enhance them for both enjoyment and commercial utility.

This project to reinvent the Chicago River certainly embraces the basic premises for creative reconstruction of America's cities cited in the new book by Michael Bloomberg and Carl Pope entitled, *Climate of Hope: How Cities Businesses and Citizens can Save the Planet.*

The aims and efforts of this project are in stark contrast with the egocentric aims and efforts of those who have currently captured our national government. Greedy old men (and a few women) focused exclusively on acquiring fortunes and protecting them have bought and stolen their way to control of elected offices and cabinet appointments. They are interested in monopolistic control rather than innovative improvements of aging infrastructure or any other public goods that cost money they believe should belong to them. It hurts to know that President Trump and his minions are working to help them destroy our inclusive democracy and replace it with a plutocracy managed by a select few. It hurts even more to realize that they are following a destructive plan devised by someone who gained fame and fortune in Chicago.

While on the faculty at the University of Chicago, economics professor Milton Friedman realized that the individualist doctrines embedded in the writings of Ayn Rand were what greedy power seekers everywhere wanted to hear. He designed a program to rapidly change existing governments to the free market design and claimed it was validated by his research. Friedman and his students of free market economics were able to spread this illusion around the world as scientifically proven economic gospel. They educated and coached powerful dictators like Augusto Pinochet as he tried to implement it with "shock and awe" in the stunned South American country of Chile. The U. S. Government led by George Bush, Dick Cheney and Donald Rumsfeld also tried to implement it with a blitzkrieg of "shock and awe" in Iraq. The catastrophic results are still unfolding.

Friedman's design does work to create the instant change sought by a few. However, is comes at a terrible price for many. Torture, and even killing, are sanctioned as last resort tools to create the conditions for full and unwavering support of unregulated free market capitalism. Guided by Friedman and his "Chicago Boys", Pinochet "disappeared" more than thirty thousand resisters during application of this design in Chile. For the full details of it's disastrous effects in that country and other places around the world, read the internationally praised book by Naomi Klein entitled, *The Shock Doctrine: The Rise of Disaster Capitalism*.

A resilient Chicago has met many potentially destructive challenges. It resolved them with a "can do" attitude and plenty of local talent. This creative and constructive application of resources was immortalized by literary giant, Carl Sandburg, when he described Chicago in one of his poems as "City of the Big Shoulders". The moral imperatives gifted by the Universal Mind to all of the major religions are transparently creative and constructive. The best examples of how Chicago puts it's big shoulders to work resolving critical issues are clearly in harmony with those imperatives. Long after the terrible Trump administration and the destructive Friedman economic design have been dispatched to the trashcan of history, forward-looking city development efforts like Chicago's *River Edge Ideas Lab* will be finding new ways to build a better future.

CHAPTER THIRTEEN

THE PHOENIX ALSO RISES: REGENERATING OUR DEMOCRACY

Written by George Monroe
Published by Reader Supported News
Tuesday, 26 December 2017 05:37

It may seem that the arrogant and destructive behaviors of Donald Trump, the Koch brothers, and other predatory plutocrats are uniquely self-serving. In fact, most human societies have long suffered similar machinations by a virulent strain of Homo sapiens. From the time human beings first appeared on the planet, some resorted to force and trickery to overpower others and control most of the earth's resources for themselves. Eventually, they joined with likeminded power seekers to control common people and amass great wealth from their energies as slaves or indentured laborers.

Egocentric humans who assumed such power roles took on the exalted titles of Pharaoh, Emperor, Caliph, Priest, King, Queen, Czar, Lord, and Fuhrer, etc. to signify a divine right to rule and to induce fear of defying it. For thousands of years this pattern of human relations was prevalent. It provided wealth and glory for an elite few and abject misery for the masses. Then, about 1000 BC the seeds of democracy began to germinate. At great risk of life and limb, oppressed peoples around the world began to resist the power concentrations that made their lives miserable. The ruling Pharaohs saw their godlike status questioned and diminished. Some democratic principles for sharing power were created and practiced for a time in the innovative city-states of Greece. At other critical locations there were concessions of shared power in the seminal and steady evolution toward democracy in human affairs such as the move by the great King Charlemagne, Emperor of the Holy Roman Empire. To enhance commerce in subdued territories he decreed that common workers should be given a modicum of education. This development brought much of Europe out of the stagnating Middle Ages. However, it steadily weakened control of the masses and eventually led to the signing of the Magna Carta by his successor King John of England in 1215.

Then came the age of revolutions (1774 - 1848), when members of human societies around the world rebelled against repression, exploitation, and exclusion. The American Revolution was a special beneficiary of nascent democratic ideas that were already gaining adherents in restless bodies politic. It was a breakthrough that lit a bright light of real hope for a world that was profoundly weary of government systems based on unrestricted power and control by an elite few.

Many people in the Western World became actively committed to the premises and benefits of democracy. However, aspiring plutocrats in their midst sought to obtain exclusive and excluding control, often embracing Darwin's theory of natural selection to justify "survival of the fittest." The supreme egotist, Adolph Hitler, turned this misguided perspective into a scheme for world domination by a Master Race with himself as the self-appointed Fuhrer. The result was a terrible world war with enormous losses of life and treasure.

After the defeat of the Axis powers to end WWII, it seemed that democracy would be forever safe from such takeovers by aspiring power seekers. However, a new form of economic imperialism appeared in the seductive writings of Ayn Rand, a Russian immigrant to the US who wrote novels exalting the primary tenets of selfishness. Through her writings and media messages she had significant influence among libertarians and American conservatives. Entrepreneur economist Milton Friedman elaborated upon the individualist doctrines embedded in *The Fountainhead and Atlas Shrugged*.

Friedman claimed that his research clearly validated Rand's socioeconomic tenets and offered strategies for inducing societies to implement them. He and his graduate student "Chicago Boys" were effective in spreading this illusion around the world as scientifically proven gospel. For a detailed accounting of the disastrous results on societies that elected or were forced to adopt his free-market design see journalist Naomi Klein's breakthrough book, *The Shock Doctrine: The Rise of Disaster Capitalism*.

Those like Donald Trump and the Koch Brothers harbor the same untamed egos that drove Egyptian Pharaohs, Moslem Caliphs, Roman Emperors, and English Kings to enslave and exploit others in building great monuments to themselves. Temples, mosques, churches, stone images, works of art, and engineering projects were designed and built to emphasize their superiority and dominance.

Donald Trump's egocentric father was immersed in the Master Race culture of Nazi Germany before he immigrated to America. He had observed and used the tactics employed by the Nazis to amass a New York City real estate fortune. Witnessing the steady accumulation of wealth by his father's selfish and often illicit actions, Donald learned his lessons well. His father eventually gave him control of great wealth and encouraged him to make it grow. With the economic windfall also came the mandate to bring "greatness" to the Trump family name.

Like many other aspirants to dominance in the past, Donald Trump has met life's challenges by lying, cheating, stealing, and bluffing with little concern for the rights and well-being of those he regards as his inferiors. When Trump talks about making America great again, he openly refers to the time when Andrew Jackson and his minions killed millions of Native Americans and stole their lands with impunity. He has always felt entitled to only the best of life's goods by whatever means it took to get them. He freely admits using bankruptcy and defaulting on contracts as "very smart" business strategies to escape troublesome debts. His deeply ingrained penchant for recognition as "the greatest" also moves him to insure that his name is displayed prominently on huge buildings, private airplanes, luxury hotels and exclusive golf courses.

Where such egotistical behavior ultimately leads is predicated in Percy Bysshe Shelley's deeply insightful poem, *Ozymandias*. It was written in 1817, soon after the British Museum acquired a large fragment of a once colossal statue of Rameses II who ruled in the thirteenth century BCE. The poem is a clear warning to egocentric greatness-seekers that they are on the wrong side of history.

I met a traveler from an antique land
Who said: Two vast and trunkless legs of stone
Stand in the desert. Near them, on the sand,
Half sunk, a shattered visage lies, whose frown
And wrinkled lip, and sneer of cold command,
Tell that its sculptor well those passions read
Which yet survive, stamped on these lifeless things,
The hand that mocked them and the heart that fed.
And on the pedestal these words appear –
"My name is Ozymandias, king of kings:
Look on my works, ye mighty, and despair!"
Nothing beside remains. Round the decay
Of that colossal wreck, boundless and bare
The lone and level sands stretch far away.

When the ancients suffered under the rule of brutal tyrants, they conceived a mythical *phoenix* to express hope that their oppressor would eventually be destroyed and their lives improved. According to this legend the *phoenix* is a large and beautiful bird that is cyclically regenerated after dying in flaming chaos after an abusive life cycle and then obtaining new life by arising from the ashes.

Phoenix energy can serve as a reminder to us that we have the power to re-create ourselves and put an end to the currently negative and destructive cycle in our public life. Working together, we can activate our phoenix energy to increase exponentially the power to perceive and create. We can invent new ways to care for the marvelous planet that serves as both our home and our means of transport into the future.

The good news is that serious efforts in this direction are already under way. In their timely new book entitled, *Daring Democracy: Igniting Power, Meaning, and Connection for The America We Want,* Francis Moore Lappe and Adam Eichen document a number of inspired citizen movements to stop the theft of our democracy and regenerate its constructive promise. Their concerted efforts reflect the time-tested message of redress and regeneration offered in the time-tested message of redress and regeneration offered in the legend of the phoenix.

CHAPTER FOURTEEN

We must especially beware of that small group of selfish men who would clip the wings of the American Eagle to feather their own nests.

— Franklin Roosevelt

THE BIGGEST SCAM: TRADING DEMOCRACY FOR A NEW STRAIN OF FASCISM

Article written by George Monroe
Published by Reader Supported News
Wednesday, 14 March 2018 09:51

No, it is not that conservative Republicans are working to take down our democracy. There are no true conservatives left in the current gang of office holders that have usurped the name Republican. There are no statesmen like Abraham Lincoln, Teddy Roosevelt, Everett Dirksen, Jacob Javits, or Dwight Eisenhower now at work in the halls of Congress. Most of those who are currently holding offices while pretending to be Republicans are, in fact, hardcore extremists bought and paid for by a stealthy minority of aspiring plutocrats. The secret charge of their sponsors is to systematically dismantle our democratic government so it can be replaced with a totally new form of governing human societies based on a plan designed and promoted by an "inspired" Charles Koch.

Koch believes his plan has God's blessing and will produce the best form of government the world has ever known. He has spent billions of dollars to finance the campaigns of office seekers and get them into positions wherein he can orchestrate their efforts to chip away at the democratic legal structure. The aim is to saturate the government with enough indebted minions to render it unable to operate effectively. When a critical "tipping point," is reached Koch and his supporters aim to activate a takeover to quell the chaos and institute his divinely inspired plan.

It is difficult to tell whether Donald Trump is a "patsy" in this plan or the consummate showman whose assigned task is to create the multiple diversions and chaos that Koch sees as essential to counteracting public resistance. Either way, it is clear that the supreme leader or person in charge is not Trump. He is providing a confusing and distracting reality show but he must eventually bow to Mike Pence who has been a secret and well-financed leader for a long time in the movement to implement Koch's plan.

Evidence to support these assertions and much more is detailed in a new book by award winning professor of History and Public Policy, Nancy MacLean, entitled: *Democracy In Chains: The Deep History of the Radical Right's Stealth Plan for America*. In an interview about the book and the diligent research that led Professor MacLean to the discoveries it contains, she sounds some critical alarms:

> This is not someone who is just trying to lower his tax bill. He wants to bring in a totally new vision of society and government, that's different from anything that exists anywhere else in the world or has existed because he (Charles Koch) is so certain that he is right.
>
> (It's) Not just money. I think it's also much more about this psychology of threatened domination. People who believe it will harm their liberty for other people to have full citizenship and be able to work together to govern society.
>
> We are at a crucial moment in our history, and we will not get another chance, by this cause's own telling. They say again and again that this is going to be permanent (like Hitler's Thousand Year Reich was intended to be), and they're very close to victory.

The most important thing I want readers to take from the book is an understanding that the Koch network and all of these people are doing what they're doing because they understand that their ideas make them a permanent minority. They know they cannot win if they are honest about what they are doing. That's why they are doing things in the deceitful and frightening ways that they are.

For a compete report of the interview with Professor Nancy MacLean, see article published by Slate, June 22, 2017, https://slate.com/human-interest/2017/06/james-mcgill-buchanans-terrifying-vision-of-society-is-the-intellectual-basis-of-the-far-right.html

So there it is, **the biggest scam ever perpetrated in the United States of America: a stealth plan to take away democratic government of the people, by the people and for the people and replace it with a plutocracy designed and led by Charles Koch.**

Let this information sink in. It is not fake news. Spread the word of this terrible scam that Professor MacLean has uncovered. Join with others to help to put down the insurrection that the fascist-leaning minority must initiate to override the interests of our democratic majority.

NOTE: As this article was being prepared for submission to RSN, word was received that *Democracy In Chains* was a finalist for the National Book Award and had won the 2017 Lannan Foundation Cultural Freedom Award for an especially notable book of particular relevance to the current historical moment. In addition, *The Nation* has called *Democracy In Chains* the "Most Valuable Book" of 2017.

CHAPTER FIFTEEN

A nation can survive its fools, and even the ambitious. But it cannot survive treason from within. An enemy at the gates is less formidable, for he is known and carries his banner openly. But the traitor moves amongst those within the gate freely, his sly whispers rustling through all the alleys, heard in the very halls of government itself.
—Marcus Tullius Cicero

ARE SECRET ACTIONS OF MIKE PENCE REPEATING AN INFAMOUS BETRAYAL OF AMERICA?

Written by George Monroe
Published by Reader Supported News
Friday, 06 April 2018 09:28

Throughout the evolution of human societies on planet earth there have been many bold individuals who felt an urge to seek power and rule over others. Guided by their internal feelings and intuitions, they became convinced that some divine power was calling them to stand up, organize a loyal team of followers, and take charge. They were convinced that what they felt to be true was a special gift to them from a higher power.

According to award-winning Professor of History and Public Policy Nancy MacLean, in her recent book entitled, *Democracy in Chains: The Deep History of the Radical Right's Stealth Plan for America,* Mike Pence has been a secret leader for a long time in a movement to take down our democracy and replace it with a plutocracy. He is financed in his covert actions by Charles Koch, who has in mind an "inspired" plan that he wants to see imposed on the majority of Americans. Although it is based on the self-centered writings of Ayn Rand, Milton Friedman, and right-wing economics professor James Buchanan, Koch believes his own plan is a special gift that is different and better than any other previous or currently existing form of governing a society.

Some especially egregious features of the plan promoted by Koch with stealthy insider help from Pence are already known: voter suppression, gerrymandering, eliminating worker unions, and management of government affairs by an elite few, all to be instituted under a dark cloak of secrecy. These features, and no doubt many more yet to be discovered, are aimed at suppressing and controlling the majority of American citizens.

Maclean states that her research led her to conclude that Koch and Pence are firmly convinced they are embarked on a messianic cause. However, their vision of the good society and the government they are secretly working to install is one that most people would find intolerable. It is ironic that on the one hand they believe that regulations harm personal liberty but they are working to gain control by an elite few that will administer restrictive rules and limits for almost everyone else.

The unfolding story of Mike Pence is an amazing example of the kind of scenario that baseball great Yogi Berra once wryly described as, "it's like déjà vu all over again." However, there is not much levity in the story of a man surreptitiously committed to a scheme that belies not only the principles of Christianity, of which he claims to be a special messenger, but the oath he swore to serve and protect the democratic republic of the United States of America. For illuminating views of the messianic character and troublesome behaviors of Pence, from humble beginnings in Columbus, Indiana to his election as Vice President, see the candid article by investigative reporter Jane Mayer entitled, *The Danger of President Pence,* published in *The New Yorker,* October 23. 2017. https://www.newyorker.com/magazine/2017/10/23/the-danger-of-president-pence

By stringent design, much of what Pence has done for Koch and an exclusive group of hard right oligarchs is top secret. However, MacLean and Mayer have documented a cluster of his statements and actions that raise important questions about his private commitments antithetical to those cited in his sworn oath of office. For example, on the heels of near economic bankruptcy and with a faltering political career, Pence diligently cultivated close relationships with dozens of far right individuals and conservative organizations including *Awareness for Prosperity*, the top political organization created and supported by Koch. He successfully promoted the no climate tax legislation pledge for Koch and his oligarch friends, after which they showered him with campaign contributions. He was also invited to speak at Koch's secretive semi-annual meetings of the most wealthy and conservative political campaign donors. After "counsel" by Koch, a vulnerable Donald Trump reluctantly agreed to accept Pence as his Vice Presidential running mate. It is no secret that Koch wants to discard our inclusive democracy and replace it with something very different. However, it must be noted that he is not elected to any office requiring special commitments beyond his role as private citizen. Pence, on the other hand, is an elected official bound by sworn allegiance with legal commitments to our democratic republic and its constitution.

In his zeal to do God's work and please Koch as his economic Svengali, Pence has overlooked a major problem with his stealthy actions: unwittingly committing **treason** by *violation of the allegiance owed to one's sovereign or state, or betrayal of one's country.* His expedient machinations are similar to what a very ambitious Benedict Arnold once did to the new American government fighting to free itself from the tyranny of the British Empire. Arnold devised a secret plan for himself that he eventually concluded would not work well in the new democracy. He betrayed his sworn loyalty to Washington and the democratic republic of America by covertly switching his allegiance back to King George and the British Empire.

Pence has somehow convinced himself that his secret actions to subvert our democracy are for a righteous cause that surmounts man-made laws. In reality he is only duplicating a pattern of behavior like the one that earned Arnold a place in American history as a dishonorable perpetrator of high treason. Pence's story is clearly a tale of surreptitious infamy that qualifies as a classic example of déjà vu all over again.

CHAPTER SIXTEEN

The Sixth no sooner had begun
About the beast to grope
The, seizing on the swinging tail
That fell within his scope,
"I see," quoth he, "the Elephant
is very like a rope."

THE AMERICAN CONNECTION TO THE RUSSIAN ASSAULTS ON ELECTION PROCESSES IN THE UNITED STATES

Written by George Monroe
Published by Reader Supported News
Sunday, 26 August 201

In his seminal book, *The Way of The Explorer*, Apollo Astronaut Edgar Mitchell wrote that his view of life on our home planet was profoundly changed as he returned from a visit to the moon. Riding back through space in the *Kittyhawk* command module, he observed the earth from a unique vantage point and realized in that moment that most views of human activities from an earthbound perspective are incomplete. Composed of disparate bits and pieces, limited accounts are always missing some relevant facts and often lead to wrong conclusions and harmful conflict. In the ancient fable of the blind men describing an elephant, each man was certain he knew the entire truth. Observing a more complete picture of human activities from a distant and less encumbered viewpoint can help to form a realistic perspective on our current trouble with Russia.

As exemplified by Donald Trump and Vladimir Putin, untamed

egotism is a central driver of international conflict. Hidden from view, groups of wealthy egocentrics scheme to eliminate and replace democracies with a new strain of fascism by chipping away at democratically fashioned laws and protocols. This includes such reductive measures as appointing directors of government programs who are committed to shutting them down, cutting current program funds, stacking courts with paid off extremists, failing to protect civil rights, incarcerating troublemakers, privatizing public properties, and failing to honor legal agreements. When legitimate authority is sufficiently weak, "shock and awe" strategies including actual or threatened war, destructive trade policies, induced riots, and acts of domestic terror are introduced to create an atmosphere of mind-numbing chaos, fear, and confusion in which more **un**democratic measures can be introduced.

This anti-democratic scheme was actually created in America based on the social philosophy of Russian novelist Ayn Rand who immigrated to America in 1926. American economist and professor at the University of Chicago, Milton Friedman, embraced the social postulates presented in her books, *The Fountainhead* and *Atlas Shrugged*. He conducted research on ways to implement them in communities likely to resist a scheme for instituting "free market economics" and claimed his results validated his premises and methods.

With teams of recent graduates from the University of Chicago School of Economics Friedman was able to spread the illusion of his "scientifically proven" economic doctrine all around the world. The governments of many eager nations, including Russia, were lured or coerced into economic traps that made them beholden to power brokers within U.S. corporations. Friedman and his "Chicago Boys" were assisted in these ventures by the World Bank and the International Monetary Fund. The austerity measures required were implemented in the nations involved and led to economic disaster for most of their citizens while greatly increasing wealth for a few.

There were other disastrous effects beyond economic disparity. Under Friedman's plan, when public resistance becomes a problem it is to be dealt with first by re-education. If this action fails to result in quick compliance, threats and punishments are to be swiftly introduced. People who still offer strong resistance must be firmly suppressed. When a brutal version of this plan was tried during the reign of Chile's dictator, Augusto Pinochet, more than thirty thousand resisters were "disappeared." There were similar casualties when the plan was applied to many other countries including Russia.

For most of the 1990's, Vladimir Putin watched carefully and learned well as this scheme was ruthlessly employed with Friedman's guidance in his own country. When the smoke cleared he joined with a few newly rich elites to establish a reconstituted Russia and was elected its President. All of this was first exposed and documented in 2007 by journalist and social activist Naomi Klein in her groundbreaking book, *The Shock Doctrine: The Rise of Disaster Capitalism.*

In December of 2017, Professor of History and Public Policy at Duke University Nancy MacLean, published an award winning book, *Democracy In Chains: The Deep History of The Radical Right's Stealth Plan for America.* It exposed secret meetings of aspiring plutocrats to discuss plans to force on an unsuspecting America an updated version of Friedman's scheme created and promoted by industrialist Charles Koch. Koch was inspired by the extreme right wing economist and adviser to Friedman, the late James Buchanan, in whose view the proper role for the majority of people in a society is to serve the wealthy elite.

Koch promotes and finances egregious actions by the wealthy minority he leads including voter suppression, gerrymandering, eliminating worker unions, and hijacking voting machines. In her search through Buchanan's voluminous archives after his death, another of MacLean's disturbing discoveries was that Vice President Mike Pence has for a long time been a secret supporter of the Koch takeover plan.

A very different perspective on our current Russia problem is offered by Yale University Professor of History Timothy Snyder, a multilingual expert on the politics of Central and Eastern Europe. His April 2018 book, *The Road To Unfreedom:Russia, Europe, America* documents in detail the kind of government that wealthy Russian oligarchs would like to reestablish in Russia and internationally.

As leader of this power group, Putin promotes serious changes in governments around the world to make them more compatible with the current Russian regime. His wish list includes elimination of democracies, privatization of all public properties, white male rule, greater access to money and power, disbanding NATO, formation of a coalition of Eurasian nations, freedom to collude with other oligarchs around the world, and permanent control of the masses.

How does this relate to Putin's courtship with Trump and messing with elections in America? Putin believes that he can achieve what he and the Koch led U.S. oligarchs want by helping Trump and his minions force the updated Friedman scheme on the United States.

A comprehensive view of global events should alert us to Nancy MacLean's warning that "we are at a crucial moment in our history and we will not get another chance. They say again and again that this going to be permanent (like Hitler's Thousand Year Reich was intended to be), and they're very close to victory."

CHAPTER SEVENTEEN

DEMOCRATIC GOVERNMENTS ARE FOREVER SUBJECT TO ATTACK BY ELITES OBSESSED WITH SUBJUGATION AND CONTROL

Article Written by George Monroe
Published by Reader Supported News
Saturday, 26 January 2019 12:27

Not all holders of extraordinary wealth are anti-social and dangerous for democracy. However, the obsessive drive for power and control of some wealthy elites comes with little or no sense of connection to other people except for opportunities to exploit them. Their egocentric orientation to life and other human beings makes them staunch enemies of inclusive democratic governments.

Current moves to destroy democracies worldwide are maneuvers that have been more than fifty years in the making and are similar to actions that led to World Wars I and II. A new league of power-seeking elites believe that a plan for political change based on research conducted around the world by American Economist Milton Friedman will finally enable them to succeed. A growing number recent publications shed new light on their attacks against American Democracy.

In December of 2017, Professor of History and Public Policy at Duke University Nancy MacLean published *Democracy In Chains: The Deep History of The Radical Right's Stealth Plan for America* detailing the private planning of elites to impose on America an updated version of the Friedman scheme promoted by wealthy Industrialist Charles Koch. Secretive planning led by Koch was based on pronouncements of his adviser, right wing economist James Buchanan, who believed and taught that the proper role of the majority in a society is to serve wealthy elites.

On November 20, 2018, ALTERNET published an expository article by American and Canadian scholar and cultural critic Henry Giroux on destructive tactics of the current phalanx of power and control seeking elites. https://www.alternet.org/2018/11/donald-trumps-endless-lying-meant-undermine-free-thought-and-democracy-and-lead-us-fascism/?src=newsletter1098070 Giroux reveals that public discourse has been debased in ways that lead to distortion, ignorance, fakery, and mistrust. Public denigration of any dissenters and veiled threats promote a formative culture of fear leading to unbridled racism and indifference to rampant criminality at the highest levels of government. The following quote from his article illuminates the destructive inroads made by stealthy operations of elites that already threaten our democracy: "The endless lying is about more than diversion or a perpetual motion machine of absurdist theater. It is also about creating a mediascape where morality disappears and a criminogenic culture of thuggery, corruption, white supremacy and violence flourishes – and democracy dies."

In April of 2018, Yale University Professor of History Timothy Snyder, a multilingual expert on the politics of Central and Eastern Europe, published *The Road To Unfreedom: Russia, Europe, America,* documenting in detail the kind of government wealthy Russian oligarchs have re-established in Russia and want to promote in other countries around the world, especially in the United States of America with the help of Donald Trump and other wealthy American power seekers.

Creating major diversions to refocus a nation's attention and energy was a favorite trick of Hitler and the Nazis in prewar Germany. The burning of the Reichstag and the terror of Kristallnacht (Night of Broken Glass) were two prominent examples. Bombarding the media with fake news to divert attention from the stealthy takeover of the German government was another tactic. The refocus of attention and anxious concern is now being successfully employed by Trump and his minions to distract Americans by inflaming racism, nationalism and xenophobia while inducing an epidemic of myopia that overlooks the weakening of democratic and legal norms. The time to expose and oppose the assault on our democracy is slipping away. Trump and his cabinet are already working to diminish the efficacy of the nation's established laws and norms. Executive branch officials are appointed as directors of government agencies not with the goal to further the original mandates of their office but to weaken and destroy them. Many laws are being violated or deliberately ignored, including those prohibiting public lands and Native American resources from being sold to private interests. Counteractions must be undertaken quickly to avoid reaching a tipping point at which the rule of law and democratic freedoms are lost for many future generations.

What we must do as a country to confront the emergency we face is to: (1) expose the goals and tactics of power and control seeking elites, (2) block all efforts to destroy the rule of law, (3) strengthen creative, constructive, and protective features of democracy, (4) cooperate with elected officeholders who work for the good of all citizens, and (5) repair the integrity of our elections which have been distorted by gerrymandering, voter suppression and electronic vote manipulation to shift elections to undemocratic and privately supported interests.

Resources are now available that offer opportunities to volunteer for active participation in these vital efforts:

- INDIVISIBLE is a nationwide grass roots organization of volunteers that works to protect the waning integrity of our voting processes and get citizens mobilized to vote.
- ACLU *People Power* is a special project of the American Civil Liberties Union for organizing grass roots volunteers across the country to resist attacks on civil liberties and the rule of law.
- *The Trust for Public Land* invites volunteers to help educate the public about the threats to our public lands and to work for revitalization of The Land and Water Conservation Fund.

A growing number of other organizations are being developed to offer volunteers constructive ways to protect and strengthen our American Democracy.

CHAPTER EIGHTEEN

BUILDUP OF PRIVATELY FINANCED AND CONTROLLED PARAMILITARY UNITS: IMPLICATIONS FOR AMERICAN DEMOCRACY

Article written by George Monroe
Published by Reader Supported News
Sunday, 17 March 2019 09:39

Barely mentioned in the media, there is a steadily increasing number of organized groups within our country that have immediate access to assault weapons and "surplus" military equipment. These units of heavily armed and well-trained combatants are beyond the awareness of most ordinary citizens. They are privately organized, financed, and controlled by wealthy oligarchs recently exposed as staunch enemies of democracy.

Foremost among these privatized, combat-ready organizations is a powerful derivative of Blackwater International, a parallel corporate army that the Bush/Cheney Administration spent hundreds of millions of public dollars to develop. Operating beyond the bounds of normal legal constraints, the well-trained mercenaries were led by Eric Prince, a former Navy Seal who had turned military privateer. Prince and his paramilitary legions were involved deeply in providing support to U.S. military personnel as they invaded Iraq.

However, a squad of armed Blackwater contractors gunned down seventeen unarmed civilians at the Nisour traffic circle in Baghdad; an FBI inquiry found later that fourteen of the deaths were unjustified. After these painful convictions and paying enormous fines, Prince sold the company. He then reorganized the most basic elements of Blackwater International into a new company called Xe Services. Under this banner for the past seven years, he has provided investment and paramilitary solutions for oligarchs and despots at locations around the world.

The concern with Prince at this point in time is that he is secretly maneuvering to regain his status in the U. S. as a warrior for the free market governance that he and his sister, Betsy DeVos, fervently believe should replace all democracies. With Betsy in the White House as the Secretary of Education, Prince is seeking access to President Donald Trump and a chance to gain his support for a lucrative plan to privatize the Afghan war.

To better understand Prince and his messianic belief in the primacy of free market economics with no compromises allowed, it is helpful to read the article published by Forbes in April of 2018, entitled *Blackwater's Dark Prince Returns*. Written by Editor Noah Hirsch, it details the threat to our democracy by Prince and his reconstituted mercenary army now waiting in the wings for the opportunity to help Trump refocus American politics: https://www.forbes.com/return-of-erik-prince/#569a806d50aa

In 2017, the Southern Poverty Law Center (SPLC) found that the number of armed and angry hate groups scattered about the country rose to 954 from 917 the prior year, an increase of 4 percent. Neo-Nazi groups within the white supremacist movement grew 22 percent from 99 to 121. Anti-Muslim groups rose for the third straight year to 114. During the year 2017, the number of anti-immigrant groups shot up from 14 to 22. In their Spring 2019 Intelligence Report, SPLC provides evidence that the total number of hate groups across the U.S. had risen to 1,020 at the time of publication.

It is important to keep in mind that these are paramilitary groups of heavily armed men who call themselves "weekend warriors." They practice training exercises and simulated warfare in secluded locations all around the country. Some are trained and battle-seasoned veterans with U.S. military experience. They are ultra-loyal supporters of President Donald Trump and have vowed to come out fighting if he is arrested or impeached. They are constantly goaded to "righteous" anger by right-wing media personalities like Ted Nugent, Rush Limbaugh, Lou Dobbs, Sean Hannity, Laura Ingraham and some deluded evangelical preachers who claim to speak for God.

At various times these dedicated warriors show up at public gatherings, shout racist comments and threaten to harm the peaceful participants.

Confrontations like this often result in violence and sometimes even death. For example, in August 2017 there was a vicious beating of an unarmed man and the killing of a peaceful woman at a white nationalist rally being held in Charlottesville, Virginia. These groups have the motivation and potential to do harm to anyone who gets in their way as they commit mayhem to help Trump "make America great again."

The formation of Immigration Customs Enforcement (ICE) personnel and equipping them with combat level weapons has resulted in a rapidly growing number of Trump loyalists that constitute a kind of private army. They are neither authorized or controlled by Congress. At Trump's command they search for his enemies and brutally make them "disappear" with imprisonment and deportation. In this role they provide another rough and ready military force at his disposal that he can command without normal oversight.

Trump has now ordered an additional 3750 soldiers to be moved to the U.S. Mexican border. These are heavily armed combat-ready military personnel with combat ready firepower at their disposal to do whatever they are ordered to do. According to estimates by the Department of Defense, this will make a total of 4,350 troops on hand to secure the border from possible invasion by a few hundred unarmed civilians. The exorbitant size and expense of this maneuver, compared to the actual threat, seems to be preparation to (as they say down south) "kill a piss ant with an elephant gun." It raises a serious question about what is the real purpose for bringing such heavy firepower to this border location. Is there, in fact, an ulterior motive for doing it that transcends Trump's ego-driven need to show the world what power he has and what he alone can do at will?

The National Rifle Association was founded as an organization committed for providing positive benefits to legitimate gun fanciers and hunters. Karl Frederick, NRA president in 1934, stated before congress in support of national firearms legislation "I do not believe in the general promiscuous toting of guns. I think it should be sharply restricted and only under licenses." Four years later, the NRA backed the Federal Firearms Act of 1938.

For more than forty years the NRA focused mainly on sportsmen, hunters, and target shooters. It supported the Gun Control Act of 1968 (GCA), to federally license gun dealers and establish restrictions on certain kinds of firearms. However, in 1975 it made a sharp turn and began to focus more on politics. After 1977, the focus of the organization moved strongly to the right and coalitions with conservative politicians, mostly Republicans, were formed. At the 1991 national convention, an NRA staff lobbyist, Wayne LaPierre, was named Executive Vice president. Under his leadership the organization redoubled its lobbying efforts and by 1998 became one of the biggest spenders in our congressional elections. In 2016 the NRA reported spending more than $30,000,000 in support of Donald Trump.

Investigations by the FBI and Special Counsel Robert Mueller have resulted in legal indictments of Russian agents on charges of collusion with the NRA to influence U.S. politics. Also, findings of the Senate Judiciary Committee indicated that the Russians surreptitiously used the NRA as a means of accessing and assisting Trump and his campaign. The critical thing to understand and share is that the original NRA was a positive and pro-democracy organization that was stolen by right-wing extremists to serve an anti-democratic purpose.

No doubt it is disturbing to learn that we have within the U.S. many loosely connected groups of heavily armed military personnel that are mostly loyal to Trump and without much public awareness or congressional oversight. Among these live pockets of potential threat to our democratic republic are: remnants of Blackwater International reformulated into Xe, hundreds of armed white supremacy hate groups looking for a fight, increasing numbers of Trump loyalist ICE troops, a renegade NRA committed to paramilitary proliferation, and more than four thousand regular duty soldiers.

These forces are available easily and they are potentially ready for a joint takeover mission. They could be ordered into battle by a commander who clearly lacks understanding or serious concern for the terrible destruction that would be unleashed, especially if media hawks say he must stay on course to make America great again. The wise counsel contained in the ancient proverb: "forewarned is forearmed" certainly offers direction for appropriate citizen action under the circumstances.

Sharing this awareness widely is the best tool we have to track and put the brakes on the steady movement toward a potential tipping point where our democracy goes down in flames. We need to find highly efficient ways to get this information the widest possible exposure in the media. Reposting this article everywhere possible is a good place to start. Writing terse comments to be quoted or referenced in journals and magazines can offer seminal opportunities to share the facts. Encouraging organizations like *Indivisible* and *ACLU People Power* to inform their active members can reach millions. Gathering together with others over snacks and beverages, or even a planned dinner, to brainstorm how to raise public awareness can stimulate creative ideas about how to share this vital information where it counts.

CHAPTER NINETEEN

Their final objective, toward which all of their deceit is directed, is to capture political power so that, using the power of the state and the power of the market simultaneously they may keep the common man in eternal subjection.

— Henry A. Wallace

ROBBER BARONS REDUX: POWERFUL OLIGARCHS TEAM UP TO USURP AMERICAN DEMOCRACY

Article written by George Monroe
Published by Reader Supported News
Tuesday, 07 May 2019 10:17

How did America's image change from being a spiritually-inspired "light unto the world" to that of a pariah nation focused on bullying fear and exploitation? What happened to slowly erode belief in our democratic values? How did our election processes get so badly corrupted? When did our Constitution and moral imperatives cease to function as guides for making decisions about the general welfare? Why did we start to feel sadness, shame and anger at news of our President's behavior and alliances? There are answers to these questions that have long been buried in deliberate secrecy. This article exposes some of the most egregious people and behaviors that have put us in serious danger of losing our beloved democracy.

There are some wonderful attributes of the United States of America that I have proudly witnessed over the past fifty years. Today, I deeply mourn the loss of many of them in our memories and social discourse. Some examples that touch me deeply are: an exalted image of the United States based on principled and compassionate strength; developing nations inviting a former U.S. President to teach them democratic procedures and monitor elections; our Constitution regarded as divinely inspired; thinking people everywhere viewing our democratic republic as something desirable to emulate; generous financial support being provided for public education; schools focused on teaching children to be critical thinkers; civic benefits and responsibilities of democracy taught at all grade levels; the foibles and gains of our history compassionately exhumed and studied; our country regarded around the world as a champion of civil rights; a grateful post-war world holding American fighting men in high regard; a grateful nation bestowing many benefits on its victorious warriors with provisions of the GI Bill; men and women educated under the GI Bill contributing ideas and labor worth many times the expense of providing those benefits; young people proudly marching in Macy's Thanksgiving Day parades showcasing the hard work and accomplishments of middle class families.

All of these excellent things occurred while our nation recovered from the terrible death and destruction of WWII. The general mood in our country was upbeat, innovative, and generous. It felt exceptionally good to be a U.S. citizen. At the same time, however, a small group of individuals obsessed with money and power vowed to destroy the nascent democracy that they felt was standing in their way. This article seeks to shed light on what has happened since that decision was made, expose those who are responsible for the losses we are feeling, and offer some suggestions for turning back the assault.

In her deeply researched and groundbreaking book first published in 2016, *Dark Money: The Hidden History of the Billionaires Behind the Rise of the Radical Right,* Jane Mayer lays bare the story of influential interlocking organizations secretly created by the Koch brothers to fundamentally alter the American political system. She illuminates the history of an elite group of plutocrats, headed by the Kochs, the Scaifes, the Olins, and the Bradleys, who have financed a plan to systematically eliminate our democracy and give wealthy elites control of the government. This book is a must-read for understanding their plan to force acceptance of a free-market design based on economics research conducted around the world by American economist Milton Friedman.

Mayer's book also provides a deep look into the family background and formative experiences of Charles Koch who has emerged as the inspired leader of the group that Mayer calls the New American Oligarchy. From interviews with family acquaintances, former employees, and reading the official corporate history of Koch Industries she details the development of a family obsessively focused on acquiring money and power. Fred Koch, the stern patriarch and father of four boys, including Charles, learned early from painful experiences with the prevailing power structures that to succeed one must fight hard with no holds barred. As one long time family employee told Mayer, "they believe justice can be bought, and the rules are for chumps."

This viewpoint and evidence of how it led to great prosperity was drummed into his sons by the harshly "toughening" lessons Fred provided. Fred Koch's rule was absolute, and his idea of punishment was physical, with bare hands, sticks, or leather belts. Another family member told Mayer "Fred wasn't around much but when his sons misbehaved, they really got it." Although it isn't possible to verify that their early experience with such harsh authority is the root cause of their current preoccupation with freedom from external control, it is interesting to note that they are running behemoth businesses over which they exert absolute control and simultaneously promote stealthy movements against democracy.

Sometime during the year 2000, brothers Charles and David Koch convened a gathering of like-minded plutocrats to develop a long-range plan to shift national public policy to the right. The plan was to have three areas of focus: (1) educating grass roots activists, (2) influencing politics, and (3) buying media outlets. Although they were best known for funding conservative causes and conservative politicians, the Koch brothers had not been much involved with media ownership before this meeting. Afterward, they moved out strongly to promote investing in media purchases as a promising new way to influence public thinking and political support.

According to an article written by Sasha Chavkin and published in the April 22, 2013 issue of the Columbia Journalism Review (CJR), entitled *The Koch Brothers' Media Investment,* Charles and David helped to launch and finance the Franklin Center for Government and Public

Integrity. It gave them a substantial journalistic outlet for their own vision of straightforward, issues-oriented journalism. The Center claimed strict journalistic integrity in exposing misuse of public funds and shady dealings of public officials. At the same time, it was found to "occasionally blur reporting and opinion to go beyond the facts of its findings."

With the Franklin Center in operation, the Koch brothers were in a prime position to influence public acceptance of a plan that would eliminate our democracy and replace it with a plutocracy managed by wealthy elites. It also set the stage for two of the most wealthy and powerful men in the world to see great benefits in joining their forces for a pincers-type movement against those who would resist the assault on democracy. Enter, stage right: media mogul Rupert Murdoch, who has a sordid history of buying and using media outlets to advance a far-right ideology that is akin to the plan being promoted by Charles Koch.

An article written by Australia's 26th Prime Minister Kevin Rudd that appeared in The Sydney Morning Herald on August 27, 2018, entitled *Cancer Eating at the Heart of Australian Democracy*, reveals all that is necessary to understand Murdoch's use of the media as a tactical weapon against democracy. The following excerpts from Rudd's article describe Murdoch's media actions in Australia and Britain that earned him strong disapproval and resulted in government sanctions:

> Murdoch operates as a political party, acting in pursuit of clearly defined commercial interests, in addition to his far-right ideological world-view.
>
> In Britain, Murdoch made Brexit possible because of the position taken by his papers. In the United States, Murdoch's Fox News is the political echo chamber of the far right, which enabled the Tea Party and then the Trump party to stage a takeover of the Republican Party. Murdoch has campaigned for decades in support of tax cuts for the wealthy, killing action on climate change and destroying anything approximating multiculturalism.
>
> What's unique about Australia is Murdoch owns two-thirds of the country's print media. No other democracy has anything approaching his effective media monopoly.

Murdoch moved from Australia to Britain in 1968 and bought the *News of the World*, Britain's biggest newspaper. Also, he scooped up the ailing *Sun* newspaper which he remarketed with a sex and sensation formula that made it the biggest selling newspaper in the country. His personal fortune grew exponentially. However, both of his papers were frequently accused of biased political manipulation and distortion of the news to insure that his political allies won elections. When British lawmakers passed laws in 1995 limiting how much of the media one company can control, he angrily closed down one ailing newspaper and moved the center of his business operations to America where he bought 20th Century Fox and established America's fourth television network.

Murdoch has always put his business interests first, taking huge gambles and creating whole new industries. In the process, however, his opponents claimed he manipulated governments, lowered standards, and sidestepped regulations, in order to to become the world's first truly global media mogul. In 2010, based on wealth and media ownership, he was ranked by business magazine Forbes as the 13th most powerful man in the world. A year later, thought to be worth around $6.3 billion, he was ranked as the 117th wealthiest person in the world.

As the sole owner of Twentieth Century Fox and its media outlets Murdoch was in a position to control its media messages. He was able to do that through his influence with Roger Ailes, the iron-handed creator and President of Fox News whose political views and tactics resonated strongly with those of his powerful employer. Ailes' arrangement with Murdoch was a Faustian bargain that did produce Fox News, the very powerful and pervasive tool for influencing public opinion toward the right that his boss expected. However, his demeaning treatment of office staff gained him many enemies. Eventually, a successful lawsuit by women employees he abused when they resisted his demand for sexual favors caused Murdoch to publicly dethrone him.

Before his ignominious downfall, Ailes worked with Roger Stone and other devoted minions of the Murdoch/Koch empires to elect Donald Trump President of the United States. Trump's task, assumed or assigned, is to take down the present government piece by piece, including the democratic features of the law, so that wrongdoing by himself and other elites have no boundaries and statutory punishments can be avoided.

His appointees to White House Staff and government program positions understand and accept the unwritten charge their boss expects them to loyally exercise. The goal is not to simply lock-in a controlling majority party. It is the total elimination of all representative parties and their restrictive democratic rules and laws.

In December of 2017, the HuffingtonPost published an article updated and resubmitted by Robert Greenwald, founder and President of Brave New Films (BNF) entitled, *What Rupert Murdoch and the Koch Brothers Have In Common. https://www.huffingtonpost.com/robert-greenwald/what-rupert-murdoch-and-t_b_898378.html*

It was first published in July of 2011, to announce the release of a bold new film, *Koch Brothers Exposed*, a revealing documentary about the corruption and pooling of power by the Murdoch and Koch empires for replacing our democracy with a plutocracy managed by elites. *On May 20, 2014,* BNF re-released an updated version of the film. It continued where the original film left off, by looking into how the Koch Brothers sponsored the Citizens United decision of the Supreme Court, and used that move to broaden their hold on American politics. The film is an astounding must-see. It will chase the darkness away with bright light and give viewers a measure of power to **help** stop the wanton destruction barreling down upon our beloved country.

Help is the right word here because individual awareness is not powerful enough to get the job done. It must be done by millions working together to form a grass-roots based power great enough to stop the stealthy machinations of the Murdoch and Koch empires to destroy our democracy. It must have the ability to pass legislation for holding Fox News, and other corporate media giants liable when they engage in deliberate lies and distortions of the truth. A lot of (real) truth is now available, but not on Fox News. Share this article as widely as you can. Exercise your creativity to bring it respectfully to the attention of thoughtful people deluded and disenfranchised by Fox News. It won't be easy, and the information will not always be graciously received, but uplifted awareness on a wide basis is absolutely essential to save our democracy. Suggest that they see the documentary, *Koch Brothers Exposed*. It is now available free at You Tube.com.

CHAPTER TWENTY

RESEARCH INDICATES COMPUTERIZED ELECTION THEFT IS BEING USED TO DESTROY OUR DEMOCRACY

Article written by George Monroe
Published by Reader Supported News
Tuesday, 04 June 2019 18:19

The democratic republic of the United States of America is teetering on the brink of extinction by eliminating the Constitution and the rule of law it undergirds. A small number of determined oligarchs, including wealthy industrialist Charles Koch are secretly working to take down our democracy and replace it with a scheme of free market economics managed only by elites. Koch is one of the originators of The American Legislative Exchange Council (ALEC), a non-profit organization of conservative state legislators and private sector representatives that draft and share plans for state level legislation favoring corporate interests and elimination of government regulations. Proponents of ALEC exert heavy influence on legislative and administrative actions in the country. Under the pressure of that influence, pieces of our current government are being dismantled or defunded so they are unable to perform as intended by previously established law. In some cases, the existing laws are just willfully ignored. Unqualified people are summarily appointed to fill government positions and administer programs affecting the major corporations they are supposed to assist and supervise. Biased loyalty of an increasing number of judges, congressmen, and governors continues to be readily purchased by generous gifts of campaign funds to ensure that they win elections. The aspiring plutocrats involved have always resorted to dirty tricks to influence voters. What's new and very distressing is the theft of elections by the use of computerized voting machines.

During the Age of Revolution (1774 – 1848), great movements of people in societies around the world rebelled against repression, exploitation, and exclusion. The revolution of the North American Colonies from control and exploitation by King George III and his British Empire drew strong support from others in distress. The founding fathers of the United States of America were much inspired by the successful examples of inclusive governance long in effect by their indigenous neighbors. They adapted the inspiring methods they witnessed in the native societies to create a totally new form of government of, by, and for the people it served. This let them avoid repeating the fatal errors made by leaders of other revolutions that, without models for a more inclusive form of governing, soon reverted to business as usual. Thus, the unique democratic republic of the United States of America became a "light unto the world" that offered exhilarating hope to multitudes everywhere yearning to be free. Inheritors of a struggling revolution in France expressed their fervent hope that it would lead the way for a better future for everyone. They expressed their deep gratitude by gifting the newly hatched democratic experiment in North America with the iconic Statue of Liberty that was installed in a joint French/American ceremony on Liberty Island in New York harbor.

Meanwhile, the displaced oligarchs in the new republic planned ways to bring down the democratic triumph and restore monopoly capitalism. They set about devising means to regain control of the great masses of citizens (other than slaves and indentured servants already under control). They reasoned that too many people were thinking and talking in ways that might keep them free and in charge of the democracy they helped to create. The basic means chosen for this purpose was economic. Except for the elites and their friends, the country was bankrupted by using the power of a corrupted banking system. With savings wiped out and wages severely reduced, discretionary time for working people to be involved in much of anything other than base subsistence was sorely limited. Under such repressive conditions, the weighted down engine of democracy sputtered lifelessly and the repressive era of monopolists (later dubbed the Robber Barons) sprang up to take over the reins of government.

This kind of control went too far and eventually resulted in the

Great Depression of 1929. The effects were so bad for so many people that another revolution was started under the leadership of Franklin D. Roosevelt. He was a wealthy and educated person with the moral compass to reject monopolistic subjugation and to work for the swift restoration of a healthy democracy. Under provisions of his New Deal great gains were made by the ailing masses. The offending elites went back underground to nurse their wounds and plan for "next time." We are now seeing results of steady incursions into the workings of government by those persistently determined enemies of democracy.

The control game being played by elites didn't change, but new means for repressing the vote were plotted and placed in action. Some of them, like gerrymandering, were openly legislated into laws that stacked the deck against a majority that might vote the wrong way. A profusion of other means, negatively categorized as "dirty tricks," were openly employed to control voting that might limit repressive power. Propaganda was used to confuse voters. Access to polling places was denied. Properly completed ballots were "disappeared." Validated names were removed from registration lists. People were guided to the wrong location or told the wrong date to vote. Polling places were moved to unhandy locations. The number of voting booths was reduced. Malfunctioning and broken voting equipment was not replaced.

Stealing elections with "dirty tricks" once prompted Rush Limbaugh and Roger Stone to tout their trickster prowess gleefully as their approach to conservative victories. After George W. Bush was elected in 2000 fellow trickster Karl Rove sermonized: "We're an empire now, and when we act, we create our own reality. And while you're studying that reality – judiciously, as you will – we'll act again, creating other new realities which you can study too, and that's how things will sort out. We're history's actors ... and you, all of you, will be left to just study what we do." Research evidence indicates that they had secret information (voting machine controls) even then that assured their victories in close elections of national significance. It was used to push George W. Bush over the line in 2000 and 2004. Then came the unexpected surprise in the 2008 election when a fed-up public came out in droves to vote, overwhelming both the dirty tricks and vote theft by computer manipulation, to elect Barack Obama as President.

The voting machines used for elections in the United States are manufactured by wealthy (corporate) elites who allow only their employees to have access to their inner workings or to "service" them. On the claim that the hardware and software of the voting machines created by private companies are proprietary, the companies that manufacture them have been able to prevent any independent examination of the computer coding responsible for vote theft. Along with gerrymandering, voter suppression and other tactics, electronic voting machine manipulation was a crucial tool used by the supporters of Donald Trump's victory to steal the election in 2016. That is how computers will be used to facilitate the theft of the next election in 2020, unless some drastic changes are made in the regulation of our voting machines to guarantee that all votes are correctly recorded and there is full compliance with the existing legislation for retention and preservation of ballots and ballot images in accordance with United States Code (Title 52, Chapter 207, Section 20701), now routinely violated in most states.

Conducting research to uncover solid evidence that computerized election theft is a reality has been a formidable task. There has been no direct access to offending equipment and its operators. Many prominent scholars and writers have been aware of multiple smoking guns and are continuing to do their best to alert the public and the authorities. In the Reference Section of his 2018 book, *Code Red: Computerized Elections And The War On American Democracy* Jonathan Simon, eminent researcher and Executive Director of Election Defense Alliance cites the broad range of research findings and related media activity *(pages 269 - 277)*. In Study VII, he presents a startling *Timeline of Events and Anomalies in the Computerized Voting Era:2000 – 2018*. It is a disturbing certainty that evidence of computerized election theft abounds and if not exposed and corrected before the 2020 elections, democracy in the United States of America remains highly vulnerable to a painful death.

This is not a give and take struggle between concerned Republicans and Democrats for influence in evolving a better democracy. It is a war of oligarchs to eliminate all semblances of the democracy that they despise. We need to keep in mind that the underlying aim of all this cheating at the ballot box has been for the sole purpose of controlling and repressing a majority that could oblige power hungry elites to

live by rules of a democratic republic instead of the "winner take all" plutocracy they desire.

This state of affairs must be broadly exposed. Our election apparatus and processes must be taken from exclusive control by corporate proprietors. Regulations must be legislated to ensure the complete integrity our elections. There must be a level of transparency sufficient to guarantee that all ballots cast will be correctly counted and preserved. Corrective action must be done quickly, while enough rule of law still exists to enforce its compliance. Action must be on three fronts: (1) broadly raising public awareness of the truth, (2) voting in greater numbers than ever before, and (3) helping to verify the integrity of our voting processes.

CHAPTER TWENTY-ONE

Here is your country. Cherish these natural wonders, cherish the natural resources, cherish the history and romance as a sacred heritage for your children and your children's children. Do not let selfish men or greedy interests skin your country of its beauty, its riches or its romance.

--- Theodore Roosevelt

PRIVATIZING OUR PUBLIC LANDS AND NATIONAL PARKS: AN ASSAULT ON AMERICAN DEMOCRACY

Article written by George Monroe
Published by Reader Supported News
Monday, 08 July 2019 20:06

He said it best in his address at Gettysburg when Abraham Lincoln stated that the terrible conflict of the American Civil War was fought and won to ensure that the fundamentals of the new government "of the people, by the people, and for the people shall not perish from the earth." Consonant with and just as unique and radical as the Declaration of Independence in the world at that time is the view of a democratically-shared citizen control of government and of broad participation in the management of society's resources.

America's public lands and national parks are crucial elements of our national identity. In the European world whence most of the colonists and later immigrants came, there was no public ownership of land and resources. Everything of monetary or recreational value was owned as an unquestioned right by a ruling class. In the British Empire of King George III, choice areas for hunting and fishing were off limits to commoners even if they and their families were starving. Trespassing near special places where salmon might be caught or killing one of the King's deer could bring torture and/or death. Access to beautiful places of nature was prohibited to commoners and protected by armed guards. Under the radical new government of, by, and for the people in America, the most precious portions of the land and nature were to be preserved for everyone and for all time.

The plans to make public lands a unique and permanent part of the new American nation were conceived originally to preserve sites where battles of the American Revolution were fought and won. Established by an Act of Congress and signed by President Ulysses S. Grant in March of 1892, the first U. S. National Park created was to preserve and make available the unique wonders of Yellowstone. The National Park Service was created by an Act of Congress and was signed into law by President Woodrow Wilson on August 25, 1916. All of the public lands and parks of America were made integral parts of the National Park Service by President Franklin D. Roosevelt in 1943.

Privatizing by selling or confiscating the properties and institutions owned and developed by a society undermines management by its members and a crucial component of our democratic governance. When a small minority controls most of the valuable property and the power that goes with it, the greater populace loses the strength of public ownership. Under those constraints, democracy is aborted in favor of monopoly capitalism. We are rapidly moving toward this ugly state of affairs today in the United States of America.

Purchased at below value prices or simply confiscated, Vladimir Putin and a small group of wealthy oligarchs now own most of the basic resources of Russia. Putin's current personal wealth is so vast it is difficult to quantify. In a model of governance favored by fascist dictators and that Donald Trump admires and appears committed to bringing to the United States, Putin and his circle have complete control of the country and the livelihood of its people. Capitalists like Ayn Rand, Milton Friedman, and James Buchanan also expressed principles designed to roll back the "infection" of inclusive democracy around the world and replace it with a form of government more in tune with their idea that the more powerful and presumably "superior" members of a society should control its direction.

Putin and his circle of power-seeking monopolists learned from Friedman's research-based and globally promoted conversion scheme the fundamental importance of privatizing public properties when converting societies to a free market economic design. Friedman's research, quietly coached by his mentor James Buchanan, demonstrated that certain stealthy moves could wrest power from a preoccupied and unsuspecting society. It did not prove that the results were beneficial for most of the people affected by his free market economics scheme nor was it influenced by any moral imperatives. In fact, the Friedman/Buchanan plan includes punishments and, if necessary, routine removal of troublesome resisters which simply counted as routine and necessary collateral damage. For instance, more than 30,000 resisters were "disappeared" when the scheme was tried in Augusto Pinochet's Chile. This model is not about conflicting ideas of Democrats and Republicans for managing our ailing democracy. It is not about the differing philosophies of conservatives versus progressives. It is about wealthy elites and their plan for total elimination of democratic governance and the means they intend to use for subjugating those who resist.

When a democratic government is created to provide for the general welfare of people, a system of taxation is established to collect something from each to provide funds for the benefit of the public as a whole that can only be provided by communal effort. Duly elected representatives decide how their taxes are to be allocated and spent, a plan that works very well if taxes are actually paid by everyone in proportion to their use of the society's infrastructure and resources. It brings hardship to many when taxes are not paid fairly for a disproportionate use of the nation's resources by an elite few who are in a position to influence policy to decrease their own tax burden, to enlarge their wealth, and to diminish needed services for the greater population.

The reasons for protecting the unique and transcendent natural lands of the new nation, to be owned and enjoyed by all of the people, are described and magnificently illustrated in a film by acclaimed documentary filmmakers Ken Burns and Dayton Duncan, *The National Parks: America's Best Idea*. Nearly a decade in the making, the six part series "is a breathtaking journey through the nation's most spectacular landscapes and a celebration of the people - famous and unknown - who fought to save them for future generations to treasure." Copies of the original film are available from many bookstores and public libraries in a set of six DVDs with twelve hours of viewing time as well as two companion books (hardcover and paperback) with dialogue and illustrations from the film.

Besides the essential aspect of freedom provided by open access to the land now owned and managed by the people of a democratic society, the grandeur and beauty of the natural world inspire feelings of connection to our shared landscape and to one another. The American community ownership of these magnificent lands, visiting them, and protecting them for posterity has become an integral part of our national identity. The loss of the greater public's stewardship of national lands would undermine the commitment to a shared national purpose within our democracy. Now under siege by monopoly capitalists who are eager exploit them, our national parks and monuments are at risk of being transformed into the ugly remains of blasted mountaintops and despoiled rivers. Magnificent natural land forms and natural habitats of spectacular wild creatures will be sacrificed to the ruined leftovers of oil drilling, strip mining, and clear-cut timbering. Pristine underground water sources will be permanently poisoned with the high-pressure infusions of chemicals used for raping the earth by fracking. A vital piece of our national identity and shared vision will be lost.

Protecting our public lands is a steadily growing task as the Trump Administration begins to shrink the size of protected properties via presidential proclamations. *Bears Ears and Grand Staircase Escalante* are two national monuments that already have been reduced in size to allow the privatizing of their natural resources. Trump is now considering a similar move to open the Grand Canyon to private companies for extraction of oil and minerals. These preliminary moves have alerted a growing number of people to help protect our public lands and national parks. For instance, The Trust For Public Land "helps communities raise funds, conduct research and planning, acquire and protect land, and design and renovate parks, playgrounds, and gardens." The Sierra Club "is dedicated to exploring, enjoying, and protecting it (public land) for everyone." A number of organizations may be found on the internet under the banner of *support organizations for public lands and national parks*. Together we must stop the theft of the unique public lands that are critical elements of our national identity and strength as Americans.

CHAPTER TWENTY-TWO

The evil in the world comes from ignorance, and good intentions may do as much harm as malevolence if they lack understanding.

---Albert Camus

FREEDOM: THE MAIN GOAL OF A DEMOCRATIC GOVERNMENT

Article written by George Monroe
Published by Reader Supported News
Monday, 25 May 2020 16:17

The loud and angry cries of some Trump supporters, brandishing combat type weapons and protesting abuse of their freedom presents a puzzling dilemma. They seem to be very highly motivated by contrived and dangerous delusions that don't square with the facts. Attacks on one's personal freedom are eminently worth fighting for. However, it is best to be sure that what you are calling freedom is based on the truth. As the infamous Nazi Minister of Public Enlightenment and Propaganda, Joseph Goebbels, once said, "Propaganda works best when those who are being manipulated are confident that they are acting on their own free will."

Judging from the confused and incorrect responses when media journalists questioned people on the street, many Americans are woefully deficient in knowledge of what their democracy is and how it is supposed to work. This state of unknowing makes it easy for determined enemies of democracy to chip away at the societal infrastructure, including constitutional provisions and the rule of law, brashly promoting an illusion that promises great things while hiding egregious assaults on personal freedom and well-being.

There have always been some humans driven to exploit others for wealth and power. When the oppressed suffered unbearable pain and deprivation under such circumstances, some of them quietly banded together and organized in the hope of improving their lives. When their pain reached a level, wherein even the risk of death would no longer deter them, violent uprisings inevitably followed.

The American Revolution against the exploitative operations of the British Empire headed by King George III was the first time in the history of the world that a group of enlightened and well-fixed men decided that there must be a better way to live and prosper. They dreamed that by establishing a democratically equitable system of governance people would be freed from arbitrary rule by an egocentric King or Emperor. There had been many previous revolutions by citizens working together for mutual benefit which were meant to gain their freedom from oppressive control. However, after much violence that resulted in great loss of life and property, there were no visible examples on the world scene from which to extrapolate features of a new system based on democratic principles.

The British colonists in North America discovered in friendly societies of indigenous peoples a seminal resource for developing the new government system they wanted to establish based on democratic principles of personal freedom, shared common properties and self-management of governmental affairs. After many fruitless searches around the world for the information they needed to do this, they realized that a long standing and successful democracy was already at work in the northeastern woodlands of the indigenous Iroquois nation. Benjamin Franklin persistently promoted the genius of the Iroquois League to the framers of the developing American Constitution. He recommended the adoption of many of the League's practices which became the main features for the new democratic government that was for a time the hope of the world. Sadly, the greedy and power-hungry elements of the new society conspired to shut off the influence of the "savages" and confiscate their lands. For more of the long-suppressed details about this dark stain on the fabric of our developing democracy, see my 2019 book *Hidden Enemies of Democracy: Oligarchies On The Rise*, Chapter Six, pages 17 – 21.

To build a new government based on freedom through inclusive cooperation, our forefathers devised a plan for civic choice-making that allows each person to have a voice and influence decisions. By agreement, each person was to commit some of the earnings of their labors to pay for the services that would be provided, including personal safety and protection of property. The funds collected as taxes were actually a form of insurance premiums paid to enable the group to achieve the needs and wants of its members better than most individuals could ever provide alone.

The main point here is that all of the monies paid into the United States Treasury as taxes and assessments are contributions the people have agreed to make via their duly elected representatives. This collection of money is theirs, contributed by them as members of their democratic community. The decisions about how and when to spend it are entrusted to their representatives in legislative bodies that make rules and pass enabling laws. The Social Security (insurance) program started under the leadership of Franklin Roosevelt in 1935 is an example of a tool created by a government of the people, for the people, and by the people to enhance their lives through applied democracy.

When a few self-centered oligarchs want to get rid of "the government" it actually means that they want to get rid of "us" (the 99%) so we won't be having ideas that keep them from taking the money and power they covet. They want most of us to be living at a subsistence level and compelled to serve the few elites (the 1%) who will decide everything. They want to take away the properties we own together, such as national parks and lands, super highways, airports, service buildings, museums, research labs, municipal utilities, libraries, hospitals, medicines and life improving inventions financed with our tax monies because they know that without such ownership we will soon have little or no influence in the affairs of government.

For impeccably researched evidence to support these assertions see *Democracy In Chains: The Deep History of the Radical Right's Stealth Plan for America* by award winning Duke University Professor of History and Public Policy Nancy MacLean. A new and very dangerous dimension to the siege of our democracy has been introduced by the advent of computer technology in conducting elections. In his 2020 book entitled *Code Red: Computerized Elections and the War on American Democracy*, election forensics researcher Jonathan D. Simon provides substantial evidence that computerized voting machines and processes are being used to steal American elections from rightful winners.

Before the Great Depression (1929 – 1939) there was no Social Security program in America or anywhere else. After the collapse of capitalistic economies worldwide, most of the people in the United States were nearly starving and otherwise living at a subsistence level. Desperately hoping for relief from their abject misery, a majority of the American people rallied to elect a President who worked with their duly elected members of Congress to create a government insurance program that promised to improve their lives. That safety net program was called the Social Security Act. It was signed into law by President Franklin Roosevelt on August 14, 1935.

Our democratic government is not imposed on us. It is created by us. The rules and laws for its operation are means we design to solve our problems and provide the benefits we seek. It is paid for by the taxes, dues and assessments that we each contribute from the fruits of our own labors. A Social Security Program is one of the special benefits we are able to provide through our democratic government. It is a prime feature of our real freedom. We elect people we trust to define the parameters and set the rules for operating it by writing and passing related laws.

Trump and his cronies are not frothing at the mouth just to take down Social Security, they want to eliminate all of the freedoms and benefits guaranteed to working people. They want to totally destroy the democratically created government that builds and protects such plans. The real game is aimed at suppression and controlling us at a subsistence level wherein we won't have the time, energy, or economic resources to resist. If they succeed in their plan to install a *de facto caste* system based on monopoly capitalism, here are some freedoms that will be lost:

- Affordable health care.
- Social Security Insurance.
- Free public education
- Self-directed mobility and travel.
- Access to public lands and parks.
- Safe employment that pays a living wage.
- Access to technology developed by government agencies.

- Access to medical breakthroughs developed by government agencies.
- Freedom to peacefully assemble and protest.
- Right to safely strike and express grievances.
- Safe public transportation.
- Streets and highways in good condition.
- Community and people-oriented law services.
- Infrastructures in good working condition.
- Swift due process before incarceration.
- Fair and balanced courts.
- Freedom of religious choice.
- Freedom of decisions about one's own body.
- Freedom to legally choose a life partner.
- Reproductive freedom.
- Freedom to interact with other people and cultures
- FAIR ELECTIONS that create a Representative government of the people, by the people.

No doubt, you can think of other freedoms taken for granted in America that should be added to this list. Join the fight to make sure these freedoms continue to be available to all of us in our wondrous democratic republic. BE ACTIVE WITH OTHERS TO PROTECT THE VOTING PROCESS AND THEN CAST YOUR VOTE FOR THE CANDIDATES WHO WILL WORK HARD TO PROVIDE THE FREEDOMS YOU NEED AND WANT.

CHAPTER TWENTY-THREE

SOCIAL SECURITY MANEUVERS AND PANDEMIC RESPONSES REVEAL MASSIVE THEFT

Article written by George Monroe
Published by Reader Supported News
Wednesday, 19 August 2020 19:47

Monies that we pay into the United States Treasury actually belong to us. They are put there to provide for the needs of the members of our American Society. We have established laws and rules for its use, legislated and monitored by an elected Congress of citizens that represent us. Any use of these monies outside of this process is illegal and constitutes unwarranted theft.

The U.S. Treasury is not the property of the government. The government exists to manage the affairs of the people, including their Treasury. The government is legally charged to do this as effectively as possible on behalf of the taxpayers who established it. It is obvious that President Trump and his backers now consider the contents of the Treasury to be exclusively theirs. As winners of an election, they believe that their victory gives them the right to exclusive use of any money in the Treasury, and any income from the lease or sale of our government-managed properties, as the rightful spoils of their triumph. They have already emptied our Treasury and left us with enormous debt in place of the money. They are chomping at the bit to do the same with our Social Security Trust Fund as soon as Trump is elected to a second term and grabs the "biggest ever" brass ring he covets. Beyond those two examples of wanton thievery, there is an even bigger bonanza waiting for him and his elite support group. All of the properties that belong to us and are currently operating under the management of our elected Congress, e.g. protected lands, parks, service buildings, vehicles, licenses, highways, equipment, furniture, and military hardware will be available for him to sell to the highest bidders.

In recent media announcements Trump has cut Social Security payroll deductions and vows that he will totally eliminate the Social Security Program as a wasteful drain on the Treasury as soon as he is re-elected. In fact, whether this is another lie or just plain ignorance about how the Social Security Program works, it exposes his desire to distribute the monies we have paid into the Social Security Trust Fund to friends and supporters when he gains the power to do so.

Protection of life and treasure in Pandemic circumstances is a very important benefit that the citizens in a democracy pay (taxes) for and expect to receive when it is needed. Economic stimulus payments are a crucial part of that insurance plan. Properly applied, they enable the people (99%) to continue working, staying healthy, caring for their children, and contributing to a truly vibrant economic recovery. The current practices of the Trump Administration belie a hidden agenda to selectively distribute our tax monies to their close friends and loyal capitalist looters rather than use it for healing purposes.

A few more months of this kind of thievery will put them in a position to bankrupt most of the country and confiscate everything of value: houses, land, parks, bank accounts, medical care, personal freedoms, justice, and, most importantly, the rule of law.

The fundamental plan of the Trump Administration and the elites (1%) that support it is for the complete elimination of our democracy and its co-operative benefits. This is well documented in two books that provide the truth about the plan and its potentially devastating effects.

The basic tenets of the plan were discovered by Nancy MacLean, Professor of History and Public Policy at Duke University, when she inadvertently gained access to original ideas and writings of extreme right-wing economist James Buchanan in his personal office files unwittingly stored in a semi-abandoned campus warehouse after his death. MacLean shared her groundbreaking discoveries in an exceptional book entitled, *Democracy in Chains: The Deep History of the Radical Right's Stealth Plan for America*.

This book, grounded in meticulous research, provides the best original resource of information for understanding and counteracting the stealthy efforts to take down our democracy and replace it with a fascist Plutocracy. Her work provides the keystone for saving our democracy from the salivating capitalist predators who persistently stalk its treasure and power, currently with Trump as their front man. https://www.amazon.com/Democracy-Chains-History-Radical-Stealth/dp/1101980974/ref=sr_1_2?crid=2XFR41DTHNNS4&dchild=1&keywords=democracy+in+chains&qid=1597198555&sprefix=Democracy+in+C%2Caps%2C163&sr=8-2

A truly unusual "hot off the press" book pulls together all of the evidence offered by Professor MacLean and other prominent authors to provide a comprehensive view of what is now known and supported by researchers of the truth. Daniel C. Neuman (writer) and George O'Connor (artist) have created a timely volume that illustrates in cartoon assisted format the accumulated truths about the rising oligarchs and their plan to destroy democracies. For a unique reading experience that will profoundly raise your level of awareness and get you ready to take action, make a few trips through their book, entitled: *Unrig: How To Fix Our Broken Democracy. https://www.amazon.com/Unrig-Broken-Systems-U-S-Democracy/dp/1250295300/ref=sr_1_2?crid=11QD7VRYU3VFL&dchild=1&keywords=unrig+how+to+fix+our+broken+democracy&qid=1597198856&sprefix=UNRIG%2Caps%2C162&sr=8-2*

If you have paid taxes into our Treasury and made payments through payroll deductions into our Social Security Trust Fund, you owe it to the country and to yourself to understand what is happening to the money. Reading these books will give you the straight truth without partisan tinkering. As James Baldwin once wrote, "nothing can be changed until it is faced." Reading *Democracy in Chains* will give you the awareness to face the impending disaster of Trump's re-election. Reading *Unrig* will show you that the level of public awareness is rapidly expanding and how you can actively help grow it for securely electing a democratic slate by working with others via one of the many organized grass roots efforts like INDIVISIBLE, Common Cause, ACLU *People Power,* and The Trust for Public Land. Find one that suits you and get going!!

CHAPTER TWENTY-FOUR

FINDING HOPE FOR DEMOCRACY AMIDST THE CURRENT CHAOS AND CORRUPTION

Written by George Monroe
Published by Reader Supported News
Thursday, 10 September 2020 20:33

A Professor of Economics at Southern Methodist University in Dallas, Texas, Dr. Ravi Batra, has long been renowned for his insights into the forces that shape our economic destiny. His views are based on meticulous research in cultures around the world. In his 2007 book, *The New Golden Age: The Coming Revolution Against Political Corruption and Economic Chaos,* he envisions an approaching time when we will be able to move from a materialistic/acquisitioning cycle of living into a new golden age or renaissance of creative learning and building, **if enough of us work together and give it sufficient support**. He offers evidence that the impetus for big change now on the horizon might be accomplished by the ballot box rather than by the military violence and terrible losses that previously have ushered in cycles of cultural change. You can find his book in hardcover, Kindle, and audio formats at: https://www.amazon.com/dp/1403975795/ref=rdr_ext_tmb

Batra's research gives us a window on how cultural cycles have undergone major changes in the past and some positive guidelines to study and learn about how to avoid the inherent pitfalls.

Here are some things that lead me to believe we will soon elect new leaders to win out over the current political corruption and economic chaos:

- The Internet and satellite TV have brought words and images into our homes that cause us to compare what we see with our own viewpoints and values. It has enabled groups like INDIVISIBLE to share ideas and join hands across many miles to mount active efforts for protection of our democracy.
- The current Democratic Party has chosen a highly qualified mixed-race woman for their Vice-Presidential candidate.
- The platform of the current Democratic Party is focused on clear plans for repairing and rebuilding.
- There is a growing number of suburban women helping to register people to vote by mail.
- Some Republicans are joining with Democrats to resist Trump and work on plans to deal with him if he loses and refuses to vacate the office.
- There is a growing number of highly educated young women running for office and winning.
- There is a powerful emergence of young women of color and indigenous origins to be leaders in making our democracy work as intended.
- World leaders are criticizing the Trump-led movement toward Fascism.
- Multitudes of young people are volunteering for grass roots efforts to get out the vote.
- Organizations like ACLU and Common Cause are taking legal actions to protect the voting process.
- Celebrities are risking danger and loss of economic livelihood to support peaceful protest.
- Writers and filmmakers are exposing innate dangers of the Trump Administration.
- Union members are volunteering to serve as poll workers and facilitate the voting processes.
- Members of the military are openly asking for a new Commander-in-Chief.
- People are volunteering to bring food and water to others in disaster areas.

- Restaurant owners are feeding hungry people in depressed communities.
- Peaceful protesting groups are being helped and protected by good cops.
- The COVID-19 Pandemic has given essential working people unprecedented free time to think and talk about the assault on their democracy.
- The excessive use of media to tell lies that have been fact-checked and corrected is backfiring on the perpetrators.
- In-group members growing weary of lies and subterfuge are leaking truths to expose wrongdoing of the Administration.
- Responsible eyes are keeping watch on Trump's military solutions advisor, Eric Prince, and the battle-ready mercenaries he commands.
- Researchers of the truth have shown that dictatorships violate a fundamental law of group dynamics and are not sustainable.
- The words of Mahatma Gandhi, respected leader of India's non-violent movement for independence from Britain, remind us that **"all through history the ways of truth and love have always won. There have been tyrants and murderers, and for a time, they can seem invincible, but in the end, they always fall. Think of it --always."**

No doubt there are many other events and actions that you, and other people you know, can come up with that offer reasons to hope. If we are able to view such thoughts as units of positive energy, add them to the hopeful ones that are listed in this article, and concentrate on them together at/for a designated time/event, a powerful force for positive and healing influence on voting in the upcoming Presidential election can be created, especially if we can get the idea for a concentrated and simultaneous action to go viral.

Imagine the profound effect if, at a given time, multitudes of us stop whatever we are doing and focus our thoughts together for the next few minutes on votes being cast for the best candidates to bring peace and prosperity to our democracy. It is my firm belief that such concentrated and hopeful attention can have a powerful influence on decisions made in the process of voting.

CHAPTER TWENTY-FIVE

KEEP YOUR EYES FIXED ON THE POOR PLAYER

Written by George Monroe
Published by Reader Supported News
Tuesday, 08 December 2020 03:56

Shakespeare had a direct line to the wisdom of the Universal Mind. He shared it with us less tuned-in mortals in the gifts of his forever relevant plays. In *Macbeth* he wrote: "Life's but a walking shadow; **a poor player**, that **struts and frets** his hour upon the stage, and then is heard no more: it is a tale told by an idiot, full of sound and fury, signifying nothing."

Donald Trump is certainly a poor player and he is strutting and fretting as his hour upon the stage winds down. In the long run he will cease to have access to the stage because, as Shakespeare noted, there is a dwindling market for wild and crazy demagogues. Extreme preoccupation with self-promotion and grabbing treasure induces a kind of blindness that inevitably causes an evil genius to suffer isolation and eventual downfall. Power control systems grounded in unopposed dictatorships of any kind, religious, scientific, or corporate, are ultimately doomed to failure as they cut off the flow of relevant information.

Donald is not yet aware of the hook reaching for him from backstage. He is plotting and planning with a few court jesters and a mercenary palace guard to fix things in his favor. He is particularly angry that their attempt to steal the election with their usual manipulation of voting machines fell too short. Evidence of such electronic thievery is well documented by eminent researcher and former Executive Director of the Election Defense Alliance Jonathan Simon in his 2020 book *Code Red: Computerized Elections and the War On American Democracy.* His recommendation to vote by mail and in great numbers was the key element in Trump's defeat and a resounding election of the Biden/Harris ticket. The numbers of ballots cast that were subject to remotely manipulated voting machines were simply not enough to turn the tide and steal the election as planned.

Wait: don't throw your playbills in the lobby trashcan and head for the nearest bar to celebrate. As baseball great Yogi Berra once said, "If you don't know where you are going, you'll end up someplace else." This is not the time to let down and relax. Trump and his minions have it in mind to keep things unsettled by legal means and obstruct the Biden/Harris Administration until the next election. In such a chaotic situation they could win control of both Houses of Congress with even more sophisticated manipulation of the voting and machines that they will own and control. In effect, they will keep a knee our necks while the evil genius mixes up another batch of Kool-Aid for his followers to drink. Survival of our democracy demands that we get those extremist-controlled voting machines eliminated from the election process and replaced with trustworthy means like voting by mail and using hand-marked paper ballots available for audits.

Stay informed and be aware. Keep an eye on Fox News and the Sinclair Media outlets. Stay actively committed to working with creative and positive groups like INDIVISIBLE, ACLU, and Common Cause. Smoldering embers of Koch/Trumpism still exist and there is a compelling need to contain and oblige them to observe democratic rules of law. Watch for signals to guys with big guns itching for a fight, like Eric Prince and his battle-ready mercenaries, heavily armed ISIS thugs, and spewers of hate and violence like Ted Nugent, Rush Limbaugh, and the fast-rising new media purveyor of lies and conspiracy justified violence, C J Pearson. **STAY ALERT and find out how to join with others in sustained peaceful protests and demonstrations to neutralize attempts to instigate a coup.**

CHAPTER TWENTY-SIX

A great many people think they are thinking when they are merely rearranging their prejudices.

--William James

CHARLES KOCH'S EXCELLENT PLAN SUFFERS A DEVASTATING BLOW

Written by George Monroe
Published by Reader Supported News
Tuesday, 05 January 2021 03:32

Behind the everyday scenes and barely visible to ordinary citizens, mega-wealthy industrialist Charles Koch is hard at work promoting his plan for America and the world. His aim has been, and still is, to eliminate our democracy and replace it with a new system of government based on a free-market plan originated by economist Milton Friedman. The electoral defeat of Donald Trump and his hand-picked shadow, Mike Pence, has slowed but not stopped commitment to advance the plan. These two defeated sycophants will be missed by Koch and the secretive group of wealthy elites that he leads but they can be quickly replaced by others just as eager to serve those with wealth and power.

After reading Koch's new book, *Believe In People: Bottom Up Solution*, it is clear that he firmly believes the best kind of government for America and the world is a market-based formula developed by Friedman and proven by his research. The main premise of this formula is the removal of governmental regulations on business, such as emission control, formation of Unions, and consumer protection. This view fits snugly with Koch's own personal outlook and experience that have enabled him to prosper economically and likewise enable many others. Also, bringing out the book at this time appears to be an attempt to gaslight the emerging discovery of his questionable role in supporting the Trump Administration fiasco.

Over and over in this book, he cites his strong commitment to enabling others as the key to upward mobility and economic success. However, there is no evidence presented that such enabling is guided by any defined and defensible mores. The level of success he enables others to achieve is measured only by their ability to acquire money and power within a framework that ultimately results in more money and power for Koch.

In the long run, either by measured choice or blind delusion, Koch is deliberately engaged in a scheme of monopolistic capitalism with himself the ultimate beneficiary. His actions in this regard are in many ways antithetical to his claim of doing good by enabling people. Using his money and power to take away our democracy by any means possible, is destructive not enabling. Supporting people like Trump as he separates families, imprisons children, steals elections, sows distrust, and fans the fires of racism, is in direct opposition to the claim of doing what is good for people. It only enables a selected few to gain money and power while subjecting everyone else to controlled lives of poverty and servitude.

Talented but socially immature personalities can easily lose their way listening to the siren call of such a self-centered world view. In this respect, the machinations of Charles Koch and his elitist followers are eerily like those of another well-known industrial giant who became lost in a delusion of his greatness and eventually suffered a tragic fall. George Pullman was known world-wide for his creative vision and accumulation of great wealth in the 1890's by building and operating luxury railroad cars that ushered in a new era of public transportation. He was widely respected for his philosophy of enabling his workers to rise from dire poverty, even previous slavery, and achieve economic success. Near his renowned sleeper rail-car factory just outside of Chicago he built new homes and other facilities for his workers, including churches, theatres, food stores, meeting halls, parks, and sport arenas so they would have easy access to things that would enable them to live happier, healthier, and more productive lives. These sweet amenities were concentrated in a company-owned town named Pullman that he financed with huge sums of his company profits and that showcased his enlightened enablement of workers as right and mutually beneficial. All of these investments increased Pullman's wealth and his image of himself as a great benefactor.

Then came a reckoning that blew away his delusion and exposed the true value system at work that may have surprised even him: selfish acquisition above all. A severe economic depression in 1893 devalued his business and properties. Faced with impending bankruptcy, as he watched his fortunes dwindle he became wildly brutal in his relationships with the workers who had helped him be a "bigger-than-life" tycoon. He resorted to firings, evictions, wage cuts, closings, and abandonment of his enabling approach. His actions clearly showed what he actually valued most: his money and power. He eventually became one of the most hated public figures in American history for the callous ways he treated people. After his death in October, 1897, he was buried (at his request) under seven feet of concrete in Chicago's Graceland Cemetery, to prevent enraged people from exhuming and desecrating his body. Will this same kind of painful reckoning happen to Charles Koch when his delusion of the great enabler is revealed to be monopoly capitalism in disguise? History will be his judge.

An article by William McGurn recently published in a weekend issue of the Wall Street Journal (2020; 10/31-11/01, p. A11) offers a hint of what may befall Mr. Koch if he continues to ignore the truth. McGurn reported a recent revelation that should cause Koch to think twice. Near the end of his life Friedman acknowledged a (fatal) error of his free-market plan, saying to his trusted friend, former NPR Media Manager Bob Chitester, "Bob, I ignored one fact. You have to have rule of law or my formula won't work." This startling confession pulls a critical support out from under the free-market plan on which Koch has formed his personal and political illusions of the merits of a government free economy. For an update on the rule of law that Friedman was referring to and to see the disconnect with his plan click on this live link for a United States Courts Overview:https://www.uscourts.gov/educational-resources/educational-activities/overview-rule-law

It must be understood that there is a cadre of very wealthy and similarly deluded oligarchs, led by Charles Koch, who firmly believe that Friedman's free-market plan is in their best interest. Losing Trump and Pence from the front line of their battle to kill democracy is an obstacle that will only slow them down; not take them out of the game. They are still very much here and ready for action. With a firm commitment to their deluded vision of what they believe is right, they continue to follow Koch's leadership to seek the money and power they want by whatever means are necessary.

When the darkness is penetrated by full-spectrum light it is easy to see that there is a terrible disconnect between Koch-led extremists' visions of themselves as righteous enablers and their continued actions to acquire money and power by exploitation of people and the planet. The news that Friedman himself eventually realized there was grievous error in his plan, should provide a compelling reason to discard it, acknowledge the harm that is being done in its name, and start putting creative energy into something more constructively aligned with the moral imperative of responsible stewardship in caring for the earth and its inhabitants.

The same grass roots efforts that delivered an election win against great odds in November of 2020 must be turned now to restoring fundamental democratic principles and enhancing the rule of law in wiser cooperation with those who are ready to work together toward a democratic government that better serves the interests and needs of everyone.

CHAPTER TWENTY-SEVEN

GRAND THEFT MONOPOLY: THE DESTRUCTIVE LEGACY OF ZERO-SUM POLITICS

Written by George Monroe
Published by Reader Supported News
Tuesday, 30 March 2021 04:43

We are quickly discovering some very important and previously hidden things designed to steal our democracy and snuff out our personal power. Well qualified researchers are uncovering the truth and speaking out despite the risk of attack by dangerous forces. Oligarchs in our midst are working covertly to keep us down and away from the wealth/power they have accumulated. Bringing ourselves to a deeper understanding of such actions is difficult, even when there is access to vital information. It can be quite disturbing but doesn't automatically rise to the level of concern that spurs action. Sharing such information with other well-informed observers can help to bring the information to a level above the fog of everyday hustle and bustle to generate new perspectives that create personal power.

Capitalism *per se* is a human creation with many potential benefits. There are positive aspects to capitalism that are of great value. It motivates. It spurs innovation. It induces commitment. It rewards creative and productive behavior. However, capitalism that follows a course of *profits above all* is ultimately destructive. Without reasonable limits guided by research and constructive moral imperatives, it can cause an otherwise promising democracy to diminish and slowly die a painful death. **Monopoly capitalism** inevitably leads to hostility. It is toxic to peace because it is exclusive and leads to angry dissent, which can result in revolution or even war. The human, technological, and spiritual resources needed for supporting the good life and human progress are thereby destroyed.

One way or another, a few people within a society are able to acquire enough money and power to evade the restrictions of established rules of law. They may attract other anti-social acquisitors who are willing to join them in an organized quest for even more money and power, with the goal of monopoly control and themselves as the prevailing overlords. Once that goal is reached, subjugation of the great majority of the society (who might resist) takes priority to be enforced by whatever means is necessary. This is the frightening situation in The United States today. Although twice impeached and voted out of office, Donald Trump continues to spearhead the burning down of our democracy and its replacement with a monopoly backed by the collective power of an elite group of mega-wealthy oligarchs. They are led by Charles Koch with flames of insurrection fanned by Rupert Murdoch and his deliberately misleading Fox News Organization. For more about the Faustian deal these powerful oligarchs have made to eliminate our democracy read my article entitled, *Robber Barons Redux: Powerful Oligarchs Team Up To Usurp American democracy*, published by Reader Supported News Tuesday, 07 May 2019 10:17.

Although it appears that a growing majority of U.S. citizens are now awakened and have succeeded in claiming a victory with President Joe Biden leading a successful revival of our democracy, there are some troublesome realities still festering. As baseball legend Yogi Berra wisely once said, "It ain't over 'til it's over." Trump continues to rally and arouse extremist groups that are committed to him as their President. A recent publication of the Southern Poverty Law Center lists more than 800 active hate groups that are primed for violent actions outside the rules of established law. The repurposed National Rifle Association has enabled its members to bring thousands of military-grade weapons into the country that are available to very angry Trump supporters. Members of ICE chosen by Trump are fully armed and operating as if they are still employed by him. There is a private mercenary army that is battle-ready and commanded by Trump's erstwhile military advisor, Eric Prince, organized and available for hire to provide oligarchs with military solutions to resistance problems almost anytime or anyplace in the world. Trump supporters within established police departments have easy access to surplus military weapons and equipment. The storming of the Capitol Building by a cadre of members from such groups offers a disturbing picture of what could be next on the horizon. There is no question about what Trump and his elite supporters want, only whether the rest of us can hold them back.

Most Americans today are already subject to rule by a government that has been reshaped to meet the aspirations and whims of less than 700 very wealthy oligarchs. They and their minions are strategically placed near the buttons that control every aspect of our lives. Their stealthy plan for incremental destruction of our democracy and its replacement with a faulty scheme they called an economic free-market was discovered by Duke University Professor of Public Policy Nancy MacLean and exposed in her book, *Democracy In Chains: The Deep History of the Radical Right's Stealth Plan for America.* Her book opened the door by sharing the exact written words of their takeover plan based on zero-sum politics.

Robert Reich's new book entitled, *The System: Who Rigged It, How We Fix It, explains* that "the real divide in America isn't between right and left – it's oligarchy versus democracy." In the book he illustrates how this is playing out in the current scenarios of us versus them. It is validated by many years of distinguished service within three national administrations. He names the players, describes their actions, and speculates on the results. A quote from Reich's book exposes a core truth about the stealthy game that American oligarchs are playing: [The power they seek] "*is necessarily a zero-sum game. Certain people possess it only to the extent that others don't. Some people gain it only when others lose it. The connection between the economy and power is critical. As power has concentrated in the hands of a few, those few have grabbed nearly all of the economic gains for themselves.*"

Contemporary American political commentator and strategist Heather McGhee's revealing and timely book, *The Sum Of Us: What Racism Costs Everyone and How We Can Prosper Together,* takes readers though a tour of the ugly realities of racism in a way that exposes historical wrongs in a new framework and illustrates how zero-sum politics in America hurts everyone, white supremacists included. She proposes that a deeper understanding of the issues and goals being pursued can actually be the key to greatly improved living situations for all of us, blessed as we are with the inherent creative and positive power of our diversity.

It is now clear that the over-riding aim of the real game that oligarchs are skillfully playing with their zero-sum politics is creation of **unfettered monopoly** with themselves in charge and most everyday Americans with greatly diminished economic and political power. Trustworthy evidence of how oligarchs are abusing capitalism to advance this illicit cause outside the law is soundly detailed in these three books. They also offer wise counsel on how to stop the use of zero-sum politics to devise such hurtful monopolies and turn our energies instead toward working with each other to create what we all need: improvement of our democratic government and cooperative stewardship for the care of our home planet.

CHAPTER TWENTY-EIGHT

BIDEN'S SPECIAL CHALLENGE: THE DEADLY WHITE SUPREMACY DOCTRINE

Written by George Monroe
Published by Reader Supported News
Monday, 17 May 2021 01:17

The hidden story underlying the "winner take all" politics practiced by Donald Trump and other power-hungry racists is so extreme and terrible that most of us can't bear to acknowledge it, although we know a lot about its malignant history.

The reluctance of Trump and his minions to acknowledge the alarming realities of the COVID-19 Pandemic and move quickly to prevent the hard suffering and loss of lives is quite understandable given their real values and covert aims. Doing what many of us believed was morally called for under the circumstances simply would be counter-productive to their hidden commitment to eliminating people they had decided were of lesser value than themselves.

A new four-part docuseries series, entitled *Exterminate All the Brutes*, based on the content of a book by Swedish author Sven Lindqvist and produced by Haitian filmmaker Raoul Peck, provides an agonizing journey through time with visual images of the darkest hours of human relations around the world. The four episodes document and explain the white supremacy doctrine with its conquest, genocide, and the myths used to justify torture and killing certain people in its name. *Exterminate All the Brutes* is now available on HBO Max and streaming plans of HULU. It provides a profound message for all of us in America about the genocide and racial injustice purposely embedded in the history of our human relations, that the oligarchs in our midst want to reactivate.

The loss of lives, property, and personal power that European white supremacists forced on the "brutes" in colonizing outgunned indigenous societies around the world was beyond hellish and eventually resulted in violent uprisings. Likewise, the treatment of the peasant classes they controlled at home were unbearable and did cause bloody rebellions. Some of them, like the French and Russian Revolutions were able to resist for a troublesome time but with no clear ideas on how to establish a better governing arrangement; the "winners" soon fell prey to business as usual. The American Revolution was the only one in the world able to change the pattern to a new arrangement that was successful in creating a viable alternative.

Our founding fathers were not perfect. They were already engaged in business enterprises achieved by seizing land, enslaving indigenous people, forcing indentured servitude, and treating women as property. They came to realize these practices were not morally defensible and attempted to create a new form of government that would redress these egregious wrongs. The result was a plan so very different and mindful of the tenets of freedom and humanitarian values that the struggling government of France commissioned the Statue of Liberty and gifted it to America in grateful recognition. Their plan was not perfect, but it was truly inspired and meant to evolve as people worked with it and learned how to make it better.

When Hitler took control of Germany in the late 1930's many Germans, especially those who had been active in a military service soundly defeated by allied forces in World War I, were feeling angry and cheated. Hitler fed their anger and desire to recover what they had lost. With fiery oratory at spectacular rallies he promised to recoup their loss and make Germany great again. He told them the way to make this happen was for the true Germans (white supremacists) to exterminate the Jews (brutes) so that the pure-blood German people could claim their rightful place as the Master Race. The terrible holocaust that Hitler and his followers created was an outgrowth of a common European mindset.

The fact that Raoul Peck's film on white supremacy exists and is now available for public viewing shows that something profound about the world is changing. The visual documentation of 500 years of racism and brutal genocide is often difficult to watch but sets the stage for considering that we now have real opportunities. to advance the evolution of mankind guided by life positive moral imperatives.

White supremacists have similarly exploited the working class in America. At the hands of career politicians loyal only to an elite master plan, they have been left behind by years of "trickle-down" economics and other suppressive trickery. Watching our infrastructure crumble and good jobs disappear overseas, the disenfranchised longed for a reason to believe that America could be "great again." Trump purposely fired up their anger against Washington and promised to "drain the swamp" while stealthily dismantling the only thing protecting their rights and needs: our democratic government. Little did they know that Trump had no real interest in their concerns and intended only to manipulate them while making himself and his friends richer at the expense of the loyal "brutes" who put him in office.

Biden is already speaking out and moving in ways to correct the faults in our democratic republic. He is in position to kick-start and nurture a creative renaissance of building and development of, by, and for (all) of the people. Patriotic progressives and true conservatives are both essential to the inclusive growth processes that he must lead.

Voters tend to cast their ballots for people and programs that they feel are most closely aligned with their perceived needs. Food, shelter, medical care, decent wages, and opportunity for career advancement are things that easily get their attention. However, the feeling of **inclusion** within a valued group identified with a powerful leader will often override these desires. Although a powerful and charismatic leader may lie, cheat, steal, and ignore recorded commitments, claiming to understand and protect the loyal members of a group against feared maltreatment by others will win their votes. Truth and logic will count much less than the **feeling of belonging.**

It is not necessary to bring everyone on board to prevail and protect our inclusive government. There will be real opportunities for everyone who wants to join in and help create a new era of creative growth and development, as Biden's plans for rebuilding America's infrastructure are realized. There will be some who can't change their way of thinking and commit to inclusive democracy. Even so, their human rights should be protected and the opportunity for personal **inclusion** should be an open offer within the established rules of law.

CHAPTER TWENTY-NINE

DEMOCRATIC EDUCATION: ANTIDOTE TO MALIGNANT SUPPRESSION

Written by George Monroe
Published by Reader Supported News
Friday, 16 July 2021 09:03

During a social gathering in the home of a new friend I had met at college, I chanced to overhear his parents explaining to a small in-group why they had decided to join the John Birch Society. With a wry smile on her face his mother said firmly, "There are two kinds of people in this world, those that have and those that don't. We intend to be among those that have, whatever it takes." Years later I learned that they routinely met and worked secretly with other "Birchers" to discuss assignments for influencing political affairs in their community. What I witnessed during that cordial visit with my friend's family was a rare view of one of the many organized efforts to infiltrate public affairs and push the election of candidates who would work to bring back full power and control by approved elites. It appeared to be a rational move that they believed was simply necessary for protection of their position and property.

Such groups have been at work consistently for many years in local communities all around the country, with the "others" barely aware of being edged into lower economic and social status. Like the invasive and parasitic Kudzu vine that is sometimes referred to as "the vine that ate the south," the efforts of these single-minded white supremacists are likewise strangling the life out of the host democracy that supports them.

The political game for a minority of self-selected elites always has been to gain and keep control of potentially dissenting majorities by

suppression. For hundreds of years the methods used were extremely violent and inhumane as white supremacist Europeans colonized indigenous peoples around the world. A new and anguishing to watch docuseries provides graphic evidence of the terrible things that wealth and power-seeking white supremacists did to indigenous people while exploiting their resources, including physical abuse of their bodies for forced labor. This four-part series entitled, *Exterminate All the Brutes*, is available on HBO and streaming plans of HULU.

It is indeed a miracle that graphic exposure of the truths that led to bloody revolutions around the world has now been released into the public consciousness. It may wind up serving as the takeoff point for a bold new strategy of education in our country that helps people at all ages to **learn what democracy is and how it works.**

During the terrible Trump era, numerous video-taped interviews with confused and angry people from both political parties indicated an appalling ignorance of the facts about their democracy and how it benefits them. The deceitful entertainment program that calls itself Fox News has consistently broadcast information twisted in ways that preyed on such ignorance and made it almost impossible to find out the truth.

It is not hard to understand why our public schools have been subject to curriculum purges that removed evidence of racism and suppression by white supremacists. The brutal treatment and killing of Native Americans while taking their land, the Tulsa Massacre and destruction of the black economic powerhouse called Black Wallstreet, the great 1929 depression engineered by the Robber Barons and Wall Street banks in New York, slavery of blacks to provide unpaid labor for profits in the South, virtual slavery of young women in the textile mills of the North, and the deadly Chicago stock yard riots of 1910, are some examples of how our lives have been affected by white supremacists seeking power and profit without accountability. Today, such overt acts are no longer allowed. However, there are some people who still seek power and profits on the backs of others albeit their methods are more clandestine.

The white supremacist minority has always understood that if the "others" knew about their takeover aims and clearly understood the impact of letting those aims develop as planned, they would do everything they could to resist and change the game. That is why suppression has been, and still is, the chosen strategy to keep possible resisters under control.

The primary aim of all suppression is to keep low status people so busy and preoccupied with their own meager circumstances that they won't be coming after the goods and privileges of white supremacist elites. Methods used range from deceptive trickery to physical harm but the goal is always complete control. Some of the methods and their effects are easy to observe. Some of them ensure compliance just as surely but are embedded in everyday life routines and therefore less noticeable. Here are some that are hidden in plain view:

> Predatory venture capital purchases
> Wages kept near poverty level
> Privatizing public schools
> Creation of food deserts
> High medical expenses
> Electronic election rigging
> Reducing places to vote
> Proprietary voting machines
> Excessive voter ID requirements
> Gerrymandering
> Exclusive legislation
> Selling government owned properties
> Feeding fake news to public media
> Restricting mobility
> Defunding national parks
> Civic education removed from public schools
> Purging registered voters from eligibility lists
> Limiting discretionary time
> Blocking Unionization

Stopping suppression is extremely important and it must be done **now.** Actually doing so will be somewhat like knocking down the rigged targets at a carnival rifle range. It will take several shots under close watch to keep the skillful operator's fast-moving hands above the table and let the innate skills of the players prevail. After this initial phase of rescuing our democracy is done, there is an even more difficult task that must be undertaken: raising the level of civics education offered in our revitalized public schools.

The survival and improvement of our democratic government depends on participation by citizens who are well-versed in what democracy is and how it works. This needs to be learned by personal experiences at all levels of study. It must involve learning critical thinking skills like those presented to the 1987 International Conference for Excellence in Critical Thinking and included in a listing of definitions offered by The Foundation For Critical Thinking: "Critical thinking is the intellectually disciplined process of actively and skillfully conceptualizing, applying, analyzing, synthesizing, and/or evaluating information gathered from, or generated by, observation, experience, reflection, reasoning, or communication, as a guide to belief and action." https://www.criticalthinking.org/pages/defining-critical-thinking/766

In addition to reading and listening and watching, which are good for basic exposure, such skills are best achieved by guided practice. This kind of active learning was being developed and included in many of our public schools and colleges after WWII. However, as wealthy white supremacists gained political power in America they began to quietly remove from textbooks any information that didn't fit with their ideas of fascistic winner-take-all government.

That negative situation is where we are today, with our tired public education institutions on their last legs before complete elimination of the kind of learning that is the keystone of our system of democratic governing. It is folly to expect that suppressed people without access to relevant information and critical thinking skills will somehow be able to fend off perennial attacks by white supremacists who want to control and manage them.

Two organizations have now realized that it is essential absolutely to revitalize our educational systems and develop an informed public with critical thinking skills and clear knowledge of what democracy is and how it works. The Southern Poverty Law Center is adding to its mission "a forward-looking program (Democracy In Action) that aims to teach people what a marvelous gift a democracy is and how to be an effective citizen member of one." The Classroom Law Project in the State of Oregon is rededicating and expanding their efforts to promote the idea that "the best way to preserve democracy is to teach democracy." The newly invigorated project members have actively helped to get legislation passed that restores civics education as a requirement for high school graduation. https://classroomlaw.org

Find out how you can assist these organizations, and/or others that are sure to follow. Help them to make sure that democratic education is free and widely available in our public schools. This is the true antidote to malignant suppression and the terrible inequities it brings.

CHAPTER THIRTY

Ruin is inevitable if our national life brings us nothing better than swollen fortunes for the few and the triumph in both politics and business of a sordid and selfish materialism.

--Theodore Roosevelt

ASTRONAUT'S JOURNEY TO THE MOON YIELDS NEW PERSPECTIVE FOR DEALING WITH ENEMIES OF DEMOCRACY

Written by George Monroe
Published by Reader Supported News
Tuesday, 20 September 2021 Godot

In 1971, NASA Astronaut Edgar Mitchell climbed into his Kittyhawk command module and was blasted on a journey into outer space. He was the lunar module pilot of Apollo 14, NASA's third manned lunar landing. For Mitchell, however, the most extraordinary part of the journey was not kicking up moon dust. It was the cosmic awareness that he began to feel on his way back home. He felt he had tapped into something profoundly intelligent and universal that could lead to understanding how the human inhabitants of the earth could save their home planet and guide the process of their own evolution toward uplifted awareness and meaningful lives.

Mitchell also realized that his exceptional ability to "tune in" was greatly enhanced by being many thousands of miles away from his home planet. The term he used to describe his profound change of perspective when he viewed the blue jewel-like earth suspended in inky black space was *epiphany*. Epiphany is the name for achieving intuitive insight wherein creative experience accumulates to a critical point and suddenly, *knowing* jumps to a higher level. He said he experienced a *grand epiphany* and was thereafter more able to explore and learn the truth of things by rising above distracting bits and pieces for a panoramic view of scattered facts. He realized that with an open mind in an unfettered environment, exciting new life Insights and plans can be imagined and then validated by employing what is said to be the greatest single invention of mankind: the concept of reserved judgement (scientific method).

At this time, we are at a juncture in our political awareness far below the perspective that we need to see and understand the swirling dynamics of what is happening and what we can do about it. Under the prevailing circumstances, we are failing to recognize the real sources of stealthy assaults on the concept of democratic government around the world and we are unwittingly playing into the hands of the perpetrators. Almost any of the fractional truths now available in our society about the secret efforts to kill our democracy should be enough to set off alarms and frequent massive protests in capitols and statehouses and other ongoing political action. With these fractional truths purposely suppressed in the recorded history of our human relations, a comprehensive state of public knowing has not yet been reached. To use a time-worn but pertinent aphorism that captures the meaning of this dilemma, **we are missing the woods for looking at the trees**.

Here are some of the "trees" or information fractions that are suppressed and keeping us held below the comprehensive awareness that could cause us to mobilize and resist the slave-like stasis intended for most of us by a dedicated group of libertarian extremists:

- A bold new documentary film series, entitled *Exterminate All the Brutes*, provides an agonizing journey through time with visual images of the darkest hours of human relations around the world. The four episodes chronicle and explain the deadly white supremacy doctrine with its conquest, genocide, and the myths used to justify torture and killing certain people in its name. These films are now available on HBO Max and streaming plans of HULU. They provide a timely education for all of us in America about the genocide and racial injustice purposely suppressed in the history of our human relations.

- Fox News is not a reputable news organization. It is a propaganda machine under the direction of owner Rupert Murdoch who has a troublesome history of abusing the media to suppress and negate democracy. The former Prime Minister of Australia, Kevin Rudd, writes that Murdoch has used his vast ownership of the media voices to sway federal elections and maximize his political power. Rudd has launched a campaign calling on the Australian federal government to establish a Royal Commission to look into the abuse of media monopoly in Australia, and in particular by the Murdoch media. Murdoch moved from Australia to Great Britain in 1968, bought up several media outlets, and continued his biased political manipulation and distortion of the news to ensure that his political allies won elections. When British Lawmakers passed laws in 1995 limiting how much of the media one company can control, he angrily moved the center of his business operations to America and set up the television network he slyly called Fox News.
- The empires of Rupert Murdoch and Charles Koch (with his brother David before his death in 2019) have teamed up to control most of the news media in America. In December of 2017, The Huffington Post published an article about this unholy alliance entitled, *What Rupert Murdoch and the Koch Brothers Have in Common*. This article was first published in July of 2011, to announce the coming release of a bold new film, *Koch Brothers Exposed*, a very revealing documentary of the corruption and pooling of power by the Murdoch and Koch empires for eliminating democracies and replacing them with plutocracies managed by self-selected elites. This film is available on You Tube. https://www.youtube.com/watch?v=2N8y2SVerW8
- Charles Koch, whose mega-wealth is based on fossil-fuel industries, has parlayed his role in the anti-democratic movement to become its supreme leader. He has established a new international headquarters of this movement in the State of Virginia, USA! Here is a revelation: Contrary to Donald Trump's media hyped power-role in the anti-democracy movement, he never has been its real boss. He has play-acted the title role in the take-over scheme, but

his actual position on the organization chart is more like the loyal plantation overseer who sternly gives orders to the field workers that the real boss, Koch, sends out to him from the office in the main house.

Through persistent and highly qualified research, documentation of these discoveries and much more is now available in a new and startling article by Duke University Professor of history and public policy Nancy MacLean entitled, *Enchaining democracy: The now-transnational project of the US corporate libertarian right.*
https://mcusercontent.com/cca23739793ff131bae0a457f/files/7855428a-b505-762c-0032-c336e7bb5222/MacLean_The_Now_Transnational_Project.pdf

Now is time to for us to bring these hot fragments of information together and realize the comprehensive truth so well documented and described by Professor MacLean: that a majority of us (99%) are under fire by a rich but fearful minority who are hell-bent to achieve absolute monopoly control. They intend to do this by any means necessary, following a plan devised by American Economists James Buchannan and Milton Friedman and applied in societies around the world with disastrous results for all but the wealthy in-group (1%). The basic premise of their plan is that people who have experienced democratic freedoms will not willingly give them up for the virtual slavery that Buchannan proposed is the rightful place in life for most of us. Friedman turned that assertion into a plan for mandatory compliance: (1) gain monopoly control by secret manipulations of the body politic, (2) invite the captured people to yield to rule by the elites voluntarily, (3) re-educate disinclined stragglers, and (4) eliminate (disappear) any hard-core resisters. **None of this plan includes bi-partisan thinking. It is only a plan for completely eliminating democracies and establishing monopoly control without reference to any moral imperatives.** The following quotation from Professor MacLean's article initiates access to facts that, if widely shared, can stem the tide of organized democracy assaults.

> "My subject is the ideas that are guiding the billionaire-funded libertarian right made notorious by Charles Koch,

one of the world's richest men. He and his brother David, now deceased, have assembled over 600 like-minded wealthy donors into the largest private political network the world has ever seen, one that outstrips in size and sophistication the Republican Party which it has turned into a delivery vehicle for the donor's unpopular agenda. Other researchers have captured well the scale and audacity of the Koch network's bid for power. What they have not identified are the ideas this network has weaponized to climb from utter marginality to breathtaking power. I believe knowing about these ideas – and how the Koch's networks operations have used them to gain a sway this arch-right billionaire project otherwise could not – is important not just in its own right, to see more clearly what is happening and why and how, but also because having that knowledge may equip concerned citizens to stop this speeding train before it is too late."

Exploitative dictatorships are not sustainable. They all yield eventually to more democratic participation in governance as people become more educated and aware. Massive revolutions have brought powerful dictatorships to violent ends in such familiar places as Rome, Russia, The Ottoman Empire, Great Britain, France, Uganda, Egypt, and Libya. There are many other plutocratic governments of powerful stature that have gone down in flames or their hold on exploitative power is currently being firmly resisted. Each round of revolutionary correction has wasted enormous amounts of life and property. Some contemporary researchers and thinkers about human relationships believe that through cultivating uplifted awareness it is now possible to move toward improved democracy by exercising the ballot box instead of violent revolution.

It is past the prudent time to rise above the darkening circumstances here on the earth and find the divine sunshine above the clouds. We need to send our minds out in space, like Astronaut Edgar Mitchell did, and pull together the fractional discoveries of qualified researchers to form a comprehensive picture of the realities in our world. With uplifted awareness we can create our own alternate plan to join with other people who are ready and able to explore and learn. This awareness can first help us put the brakes on the leaders of the transnational corporate libertarian movement who are steadily forging the chains for our enslavement. We can then use the best of religious thought and modern science working together to find morally justified ways to save democracy and improve life on the earth for all of its inhabitants. **It starts by our personal commitment to share this information as widely and as soon as possible.**

RESEARCHING AND LEARNING THE TRUTH ABOUT DEMOCRACY

> I believe there are more instances of the abridgement of the freedom of the people by gradual and silent encroachments of those in power than by violent and sudden usurpations.
>
> --James Madison

When I started to write about my experience and discoveries at the Documentation Center in Nuremberg, Germany in 2012, it was obvious that prior to that visit my awareness of the truth about the hidden players of WWII and their ulterior motives had been sorely limited. Over the next six years of researching and writing, I became aware of a world of information about the enemies of democratic government, much of it deliberately hidden. Since June of 2016, my aim with each of the thirty articles I wrote and submitted to Reader Supported News (RSN) was to share as much of the truth about the assaults on democracy as I had discovered to date. Sometimes it was necessary to reiterate previous findings so I could put the more recent discoveries in the most comprehensive context. Little by little, I learned that a few power-hungry oligarchs, fascists, nationalists, and others were developing a plan to subvert inclusive democracy and replace it with a free market scheme under their exclusive control.

Democracy in human affairs is a dynamic process. A constructive struggle between opposing thoughts was very likely activated when some primitive human beings became aware of their inherent ability to think and plan beyond their predatory animal existence. The curve of evolution toward democracy from that auspicious beginning has been long and extremely brutal at times, but it has unrelentingly trended toward human relations based on inclusive participation and constructive exchange of opposing ideas.

The British colonial subjects in North America who dreamed and fought into existence a democratic republic somehow recognized the dual nature of the process that moves human affairs forward. They learned some key facts from their indigenous neighbors who were already aware of the value of opposing views to serve as checks and balances in an inclusive approach to formulating viable governmental structure and behavioral norms within a society. This approach was designed to keep discourse open and prevent total capture of the new government by any group exclusively oriented to a single point of view.

The extraordinary birth of the United States of America was an anomaly in the world at that time. It was a prodigious departure from the way human affairs had been governed for thousands of years. Wealthy elites had to make painful adjustments and many vowed to shut this aberration down as soon as possible and get things back to the familiar status quo with a privileged few in charge.

Governance systems resulting from unopposed dictatorships of any kind (religious, scientific, governmental, or corporate) are ultimately doomed to failure as they stifle the principle of duality. Power derived by overwhelming force, shock, and awe promotes a status quo that dries up the questioning and selecting that is crucial for the evolution of increasingly inclusive governmental norms. Governance systems that are mindful of the principle of duality between opposing views can promote positive and popularly endorsed new cultural ideas and movements. Such systems provide a crucible for the frank debating of ideas that forms the core of true conservatism. They are open and work constructively for the common good. However, they are subject to persistent and often surreptitious opposition by those who would concentrate power to their own circle.

The current conditions of chaos and corruption in our world could offer myriad opportunities for progress by strenuously opposing the standards underlying corrupt practices with those that expand a more truly humane and democratic governance. Throughout our presence on planet earth, human beings have always had some raw knowledge of our tenuous existence in a world with manifold physical challenges. Because of our latent ability to learn how to meet these challenges and to seek meaning in human life, we are in a gradual growth process from a sole focus on personal survival toward an expanding and more inclusive circle of concern. Despite perennial struggles to kill opposing views that have resulted in enormous destruction of life and property, the principle of duality in creative dialogue between opposing viewpoints contributes to a more constructive balance in human affairs.

The zeitgeist on planet earth does tend to react and redress untenable human inequities. Terrible as they were, the military experiences of Americans during two World Wars resulted in an unprecedented distribution of power to ordinary citizens that elites could not foresee or suppress. Traveling to other countries and interacting with people in different cultures provided soldiers with a first-hand education that greatly broadened their awareness of other possibilities beyond those available in their lives at home. Soldiers came back more assertive and empowered to demand expanded opportunities. With the passage of the GI Bill for WWII veterans in America, working class people began to access levels of education, achievement, and a measure of equality envisioned in the country's founding but not previously actualized.

The pursuit of concentrating wealth and power to their own group at the expense of all others is a kind of blindness that prevents self-centered human beings from seeing beyond their narrow and ultimately destructive goals in this world that we all occupy so briefly. Throughout human history, the means to gain and keep power over others have been innovative and terrible. For many centuries, the repressive posture of the Egyptian Pharaohs, the Roman Empire, the Ottoman Caliphates, the Borgias of Italy, and the British Empire was effective in suppressing and firmly controlling actions of the general populace. The enforced status quo kept the general level of awareness below a threshold that could support concerted resistance.

Now and then, progressive alternatives were introduced by respected leaders who, by their charismatic words and example, called for more open and inclusive systems of relating and governing. Gautama Buddha, Prophet Moses, Prophet Muhammad, and Jesus of Nazareth were among those who influenced millions to think in more open and inclusive ways. They inspired followers with the idea that each of them had a God-given right to construct their own destinies and relations with their fellow human beings. Their teachings became the beating hearts of several great religious movements.

Unfortunately, these originally positive movements were appropriated by autocrats who consolidated their power and control, suppressed the actions and independent initiatives of the awakening populace, and used religion as a tool for maintaining that control. The resourceful Roman Emperor Constantine converted to Christianity, decreed it to be the official religion of the State, and used it as one tool in consolidating his power over his empire.

A seminal milestone in the rough but steady evolution toward democracy in human affairs was an unprecedented move by Charlemagne, a later Emperor of the Holy Roman Empire who decreed that workers should be given a modicum of education to enhance commerce in subdued territories. Emboldened by their education and the concomitant power that it offered, the greatly favored brewers of Cologne inaugurated the world's first collective bargaining to induce Charlemagne to raise their wages and improve working conditions. A gradual broadening of opportunities for education contributed to Europe's emergence from the Middle Ages and steadily weakened elite control of the populace. Another seminal move toward more inclusive government came from the English King John's signing of the Magna Carta in 1215 which expanded government control beyond the monarchy to share power with the English barons. Despite inevitable repressive backlash such as the Spanish Inquisition (1478 – 1834), a gradual evolution toward democratic principles continued as craftsmen formed guilds, leagues, alliances and other organizations to negotiate for better wages and more humane work conditions.

After the Nuremberg Trials were concluded and the world settled back to rest, rebuild, and pay attention to personal pursuits, American Economics Professor, Milton Friedman, became a widely recognized icon around promoting a free market plan for economic change by capitalizing on the exclusionary views of Ayn Rand. Her two books, *The Fountainhead* and *Atlas Shrugged,* that proposed and sanctioned narrow self-interested goals, became widespread in America after WWII. Accepting her views as universally valid, Friedman conducted research on the economic effects of their applications in various cultures around the world and concluded he had demonstrated their validity despite some disastrous results. He was encouraged in this enterprise by his teacher and mentor, James Buchanan, a right-wing economist who had collected similar data supporting his perspective that dovetailed with those of Rand and Friedman. Buchanan wrote and taught that democracy was a mistake and should be replaced by a government controlled and managed by an elite plutocracy with everyone else consigned to service roles. Like Rand, he promoted a view of individualism wherein elites and their corporations were responsible only for themselves.

When Friedman, with the help of his University of Chicago graduate students of economics, applied his free market plan in various cultures around the world, the actual result was disaster for most citizens and economic bonanza for an elite few. There was much destruction of real property and numerous lives were lost. Political unrest, corruption, and severe economic imbalance became rampant. Their plans and research findings were not weighed against any constructive moral imperatives reflecting the purpose and higher values of human life.

My research and learning over the past six years has led me to the conclusion that most of us have been "missing the woods for looking at the trees." When all is laid bare, there is a primal issue that transcends everything else: the struggle between two opposing choices of what we human beings should be doing with the divine life invested in each of us.

One of these choices is aimed at working together to create the conditions for a safe, healthy, and purposeful lives for all inhabitants of the earth, with any needed government decisions made by the many through their duly chosen representatives. The plethora of good ideas about how life issues might be best resolved under this arrangement are winnowed out and reasonably trimmed down by thoughtful deliberations. This process enables adopting the best decisions for all under the circumstances. Life goals, determined by the desire for personal freedom with the broad scope of reasoned life purposes, guide committed and active participation.

The other choice is a game being played by Oligarchs and their deluded minions around the world that is aimed at control and exclusion of others. Money and power are the tokens that these players manipulate by any means possible to build and protect the material riches they acquire. Their monopolistic game is mostly kept out of sight to prevent armed resistance by those who don't agree. There is no guidance by reasoned moral imperative.

Research evidence now strongly supports the conclusions described above. It also predicts that movements based on the choice championed by money and power-hungry oligarchs will inevitably arise and seek to usurp the power of the democratic choice before it spreads. This will result in wasteful loss of human life and destruction of many valued human creations, from art to architecture. We must be forever wide awake and truly watchful to notice early signs so the damage can be quickly stopped.

But that isn't all we must do. A democracy is not a one-act play. It offers special freedoms and life enhancing benefits, but there is a real cost to having and maintaining a viable one. It can be lost or secretly stolen without its absence being noticed until you reach for it and find it is gone. History tells us that democracies exist in the world today **only** because brave souls chose to resist bad living conditions and fight for free participation in their governance. Controlling power was wrested from long established elites who used deprivation and fear and lies to usurp the best of everything and keep it exclusive to themselves. To save the democracy we are now fortunate to have on loan from the universal mind, and be able to improve it for our children, we must make the commitment to be fully informed and actively participate in its functions—always.

Every living human being is on a journey and traveling on the same vehicle: Planet Earth. There is great need for a new moral compass to guide us in making decisions about how to conduct ourselves as we ride through time and space. We must not let a few short-sighted and greedy people capture the resources needed and unwittingly destroy the vehicle on which we all are living and traveling. Without solid moral imperatives we are passengers on a rudderless ship wallowing in a sea of options without viable means to tell which offer life-enhancing opportunities and which include obstacles that can sink us.

We need to realize that our journey is infinitely larger than our individual lifetimes. Some of what lives within us during a single life span can continue within our descendants, ad infinitum. With an evolving moral compass and moral imperatives created by religion and science working together, we can stay focused on our roles as stewards of the earth and its inhabitants. Guided by that perspective we can reverently care for our home base and support the development of technology that will allow humankind to explore safely other worlds as well. Reactivating the principle of duality in our political discourse and working together, we can invent new ways to care for the planet that serves as both our home and our vehicle for traveling into the future.

Now that you have read this book and are consciously aware of the unrelenting truth it documents, the existential questions are: **What can you do about it? What will you do about it? Who will you do it for? How soon will you start?**

SELECTED REFERENCES

Batra, Ravi. *The New Golden Age: The Coming Revolution Against Political Corruption and Economic Chaos.* Palgrave MacMillan, 2007.

_____. *The Myth of Free Trade: The Pooring of America.* Atria Books, 1996.

Boggs, Grace Lee. *The Next American Revolution: Sustainable Activism For The Twenty-First Century.* University of California Press, 2012.

Black, Edwin. *Nazi Nexus:America's Corporate Connections to Hitler's Holocaust.* Dialog Press, 2009.

Bloomberg, Michael and Pope, Carl. *Climate of Hope: How Cities, Businesses, and Citizens Can Save The Planet.* St. Martin's Press, 2017.

Chavkin, Sasha. *The Koch Brothers Media Investment.* Article published in the Columbia Journalism Review (CJR), April 22, 2013.

Clements, Jeffrey D. *Corporations are not People: Reclaiming Democracy from Big Money and Global Corporations.* Berrett-Kohler Publishers, Inc., 2014.

Conner, Claire. *Wrapped in the Flag: A personal History of America's Radical Right.* Beacon Press, 2013.

Diamond, Jared. *Guns, Germs, and Steel: The Fates of Human Societies.* W.W. Norton & Company, 1999.

Fitrakis, Bob and Wasserman, Harvey. *The Strip & Flip Election of 2016: Five Jim Crows & Electronic Election Theft.* CICJ Books. 2016.

_____. *The Strip & Flip Disaster of America's Stolen Elections: Updated "Trump" Edition of Strip and Flip Selection of 2016.* Biblio Publishing, 2017.

Gore, Al. *The Future: Six Drivers of Global Change.* Random House, 2013.

Giroux, Henry. *Donald Trump's endless lying is meant to undermine free thought and democracy - and lead us into fascism.* Article published by *AlterNet*, November 20, 2018.

Greenwald, Robert. *What Rupert Murdoch and the Koch Brothers Have In Common.* Article published in Huffington Post, December 6, 2017.

Harman, Willis. *Global Mind Change: The Promise of the 21st Century.* Berrett-Koehler Publishers, Inc. and the Institute of Noetic Sciences, Second Edition, 1998.

Hawking, Stephen. *A Brief History of Time.* Bantam Books, 1988.

Hirsch, Noah. (Editor's Pick) *Blackwater's Dark Prince Returns.* Article published in Forbes. April 4, 2018.

Houston, Jean. *Manual for the Peacemaker: An Iroquois Legend to Heal Self & Society. Quest Books, 1995.*

Klein, Naomi. *The Shock Doctrine: The Rise of Disaster Capitalism.* Picador Books, 2008.

Klein, Naomi. *This Changes Everything: Capitalism vs The Climate.* Simon & Schuster, 2014.

Krugman, Paul. *End This Depression Now!* W.W. Norton & Company, 2012.

Lappe, Francis Moore and Eichen, Adam. *Daring Democracy: Igniting Power, Meaning, and Connection for the America We Want.* Beacon Press Books, 2017.

Lewis, Michael. *The Big Short: Inside The Doomsday Machine.* W.W. Norton & Company, Inc., 2010.

MacLean, Nancy. *Democracy In Chains: The Deep History of the Radical Right's Stealth Plan for America.* Penguin Random House, 2018.

MacLean, Nancy. Enchaining democracy: The now -transnational project of the US corporate libertarian right. https://mcusercontent.com/cca23739793ff131bae0a457f/files/7855428a-b505-762c-0032-c336e7bb5222/MacLean_The_Now_Transnational_Project.pdf

Mayer, Jane. Dark Money: *The Hidden History of the Billionaires Behind the Rise of the Radical Right. Anchor Books, 2017.*

Mayer, Jane. The Big Money Behind The Big Lie. The New Yorker. Article published in The New Yorker Magazine. August 9, 2021.

_____. *The Danger of President Pence.* Article published in *The New Yorker Magazine.* October 23, 2017.

Mitchell, Edgar D. with Dwight Williams. *The Way of The Explorer: An Apollo Astronaut's Journey Through the Material and Mystical Worlds.* G. P. Putnam's Sons, 1996.

Morgenson, Gretchen. *The Capitalist's Bible.* Harper Collins Publishers, 2009.

Nader, Ralph. *Breaking Through Power: It's Easier Than We Think.* City Lights Books, 2016.

Palast, Greg. *The Best Democracy Money Can Buy: An Investigative Reporter Exposes the Truth about Globalization, Corporate Cons and High Finance Fraudsters, Pluto Press,* 2002.

_____. *Armed Madhouse: From Baghdad to New Orleans – Sordid Secrets & Strange Tales of a White House Gone Wild.* A Plume Book, 2008.

Parry, Robert. *America's Stolen Narrative: From Washington and Madison to Nixon, Reagan and the Bushes to Obama.* The Media Consortium, 2012.

Perkins, John. *Confessions of an Economic Hit Man.* Plume Books, 2005.

Piketty, Thomas. *Capital in the Twenty-First Century.* Harvard University Press, 2014.

Raymond, Allen with Spiegelman, Ian. *How To Rig An Election: Confessions of a Republican Operative.* Simon and Schuster Paperbacks, 2008.

Reich, Robert B. *The Common Good.* Alfred A. Knopf, 2018.

Ross, Carne. *The Leaderlesss Revolution: How Ordinary People Will Take Power And Change Politics In The 21st Century. A Plume Book, 2011.*

Rudd, Kevin. (Australia's 26th Prime Minister). *Cancer Eating at the Heart of Australian Democracy.* The Sydney Morning Herald, August 27, 2018.

Scahill, Jeremy. *Blackwater: The Rise of the World's Most Powerful Mercenary Army. Nation Books, 2007.*

Scheer, Robert. *The Great American Stickup: How Reagan Republicans and Clinton Democrats Enriched Wall Street While Mugging Main Street.* Nation Books, 2010.

Simon, Jonathan D. *Code Red: Computerized Election Theft and The New American Century: Election 2016 Edition.* Copyrighted Material, 2016.

_____. *Code Red: Computerized Elections and the War on American Democracy: 2018 Edition.* Copyrighted Material, 2018.

Sherman, Gabriel. *The Loudest Voice in the Room: How the Brilliant, Bombastic Roger Ailes Built Fox News – and Divided a Country.*Random House, 2017.

Snyder, Timothy. *The Road To Unfreedom: Russia, Europe, America.* Crown Publishing Group, 2018.

Zinn, Howard. *A People's History of The United States.* Teaching materials by Kathy Emery and Ellen Reeves. Updated Edition 2003.

_____. *A People's History of American Empire.* Henry Holt and Company. 2008.

ABOUT THE AUTHOR

George Monroe grew up in a small town in the southern hill country of America's heartland where his creative learning style was not always understood or appreciated. His *different* insights were often aggressively devalued or rejected by his family and others in the provincial environs of his home community. Numerous synchronistic experiences, including the timely appearances of caring mentors, enabled him to transcend these limitations and become an exemplary researcher and gifted teacher. In subject areas ranging from science to spirituality, he has always vigorously pursued cutting edge information to help himself and his students *think outside the box*. He obtained his Ph.D. in an interdisciplinary program focused on facilitating change processes in organizations. He also completed post-doctoral programs to become a Licensed Clinical Psychologist and an Approved Consultant in Clinical Hypnosis. After fourteen years of teaching and program development at the University of Illinois in Chicago, he left academia to develop a private psychotherapy practice. He currently resides with his wife, Merle Citrin Monroe, in Evanston, Illinois.

www.ingramcontent.com/pod-product-compliance
Lightning Source LLC
Chambersburg PA
CBHW020425220526
45464CB00002B/574